Praise for
Creating a Fulfilling Life Through Spiritual Growth

"The genius of **Creating a Fulfilling Life Through Spiritual Growth** is the simplicity with which Lennox distills into easily understandable and actionable steps, your ability to grow by applying the action assignments to your own unique personal circumstances. You learn not just what to do, but how to do it, making this a must-read book."

— Dr. Jussi Eerikäinen,
Cardiologist, Brain Researcher,
Mathematician, and Bestselling Author

"What I enjoyed most about this book is that it is interactive. Lennox encourages you to participate through exercises utilizing the principles of **neuro·ADAPT·ive Programming**. My favorite nugget from the book is, **"If you are in the desert and you have prayed for rain to fill water bottles, you'd better make sure you have water bottles to fill"**. Many folks want things they aren't prepared for; and so, getting them doesn't bring the happiness they anticipated. This book develops the reader's consciousness to be prepared for what they want <u>before</u> they get it, thereby enhancing the happiness it brings. Reading the book is like having the author walk with you on your journey, much like a friend."

— Charlotte Sherman,
Real Estate Broker, and Entrepreneur

"Lennox Cornwall's **Creating a Fulfilling Life Through Spiritual Growth** is an essential guide for making the most out of life, and tapping into your full potential. Lennox includes thoughtful action steps that help guide you towards action, and thinking that will propel you to make the most of the coaching the book provides."

— Jeremy Weiser,
Director, Sun City Financial

"A book is only as good as its author. Throughout his life, Lennox's experience as both an entrepreneur and a leadership coach has drawn him into situations where his capital and energy have been applied to create transformative solutions; most notably in the development of others. He combines his acquired skills in business and finance with those acquired from self-examination to create impactful spiritual growth tools for many business-minded individuals who, sometimes, previously resisted these ideals. **Creating a Fulfilling Life Through Spiritual Growth** is innovative, empowering, and entertaining. I highly recommend it, the man behind it, and his principles of success."

— Robert B. Jorgensen,
Vice President, NV Legal Docs, LLC

"Lennox Cornwall's latest book, **Creating a Fulfilling Life Through Spiritual Growth**, is needed now, more than perhaps at any time in recent history. We've all seen how the world, and our place in it, can change in an instant. Lennox provides a great, easy-to-read and insightful path forward."

— Burke Allen,
Chief Media Strategist, Allen Media Strategies

"This book is a treasure trove and will easily expand the reader's understanding of Self. It presents an exciting and fresh perspective on Creating a Fulfilling Life. This is exactly what is needed for those awakening to a higher stage of consciousness. For an even richer experience, be sure to complete the action assignments, and apply and share its principles. You'll be glad you did."

— Wendy Ditta,
Bestselling Author, **The More I Learn, The More I Love**

"**Creating a Fulfilling Life Through Spiritual Growth** demonstrates how to use your own personal resources to achieve what you want from life. Brilliantly written with excellent keys to living a fulfilling, successful life."

— Monty Meadows,
Realtor

"The material in this book is very well thought out and, if applied, can change your life. It has already changed mine. I thought I was living a balanced and fulfilling life until I read **Creating a Fulfilling Life Through Spiritual Growth**. Reading it urged me to refocus my energy towards some goals I was afraid to attain, but am now certain I will. Lennox presents an easy to follow, step-by-step process for creating the life of your choice—the life of your dreams. You are never too old, too young, or too poor. You'll learn that there are no boundaries, apart from those you create for yourself. This is a powerful book that unlocks your true potential. Needless to say, I highly recommend **Creating a Fulfilling Life Through Spiritual Growth** to anyone wanting to positively change their life."

— Brian Craveiro, Artist and Entrepreneur

"**Creating a Fulfilling Life Through Spiritual Growth** is very enlightening, and easy to follow. I especially like the action steps after each chapter. In the book, Lennox demonstrates a great ability to draw out what you truly want from your life; and, his **neuro·ADAPT·ive Programming** is the methodology by which you can get it. The philosophy is one that leads to ultimate happiness, achievement and satisfaction. Lennox is a wise man. I have passed his book onto my son so he too can benefit from Lennox's wisdom. **Creating a Fulfilling Life Through Spiritual Growth** is a book that I've added to the "must-read" list for my patients."

— Dr. Bob Heron,
Chiropractic Kinesiologist

"**Creating a Fulfilling Life Through Spiritual Growth** is the perfect marriage of philosophy and practical wisdom; and, as such, is the perfect manual for success."

— Pat Caruth,
Sales and Marketing Entrepreneur

Creating a
Fulfilling Life
Through
Spiritual Growth

Featuring the author's proprietary method for creating a fulfilling life:
neuro·ADAPT·ive Programming

LENNOX A. CORNWALL

Published by One Truth Publishing

Copyright© 2020 Lennox A. Cornwall

1st Edition, 2020

No part of this book may be reproduced or transmitted in any form or by any means, electronic or mechanical, including photocopying, recording, or by any information storage and retrieval system, without written permission from the author, except for the inclusion of brief quotation in a review.

Limit of Liability and Disclaimer of Warranty: The publisher has used its best efforts in preparing this book, and the information provided herein is provided "as is".

This book is designed to provide information and motivation to its readers. It is sold with the understanding that neither publisher nor author is engaged in rendering any type of psychological, medical, legal, or any other kind of professional advice. The content of each article is the sole expression and opinion of the author. Neither publisher nor author shall be liable for any physical, psychological, emotional, financial, or commercial damages, including, but not limited to, special, incidental, consequential, or other damages. Our views and rights are the same: You are responsible for your own choices, actions, and results.

Permission should be addressed to: lennox@lennoxcornwall.com

Publisher's Catalogue-in-Publication data

(Prepared by The Donohue Group, Inc.)

Names: Cornwall, Lennox A., author.

Title: Creating a fulfilling life through spiritual growth / Lennox A. Cornwall.

Description: 1st edition. | [Las Vegas, Nevada] : One Truth Publishing, 2020. | "Featuring the author's proprietary method for creating a fulfilling life: neuro·ADAPT·ive Programming."

Identifiers: ISBN 9780999406717 | ISBN 9780999406731 (ebook)

Subjects: LCSH: Self-actualization (Psychology) | Visualization. | Spiritual life--Psychological aspects. | Subconsciousness. | Choice (Psychology) | BISAC: SELF-HELP / Personal Growth / Happiness. | SELF-HELP / Spiritual.

Classification: LCC BF637.S4 C67 2020 (print) | LCC BF637.S4 (ebook) | DDC 158.1--dc23

Editors: Katherine Pickett, Pop Editorial Services; Simon Richardson
Cover Design: Cover Design: Solaja Slobodan
Layout: Solaja Slobodan

Contents

CHAPTER ONE In the Beginning 13
   A Universal Problem 14
   The Memories Controlling Your Life 16
   Freedom isn't Free 17
   Two Personal Revelations 20
CHAPTER TWO A New Beginning 23
   What is neuro·ADAPT·ive Programming? 23
   Why Does neuro·ADAPT·ive Programming Work? 24
   So, What is a Fulfilling Life, Anyway? 26
   Your Life is Like a Pendulum 27
   Your Roadmap 29
   Some Assertions About Being Human 29
CHAPTER THREE Existing on Autopilot 33
   Thank You, I've Got This 33
   The Most Dangerous Hidden Trap 34
   Escape Is Close at Hand 35
   Your Fulfilling Life Action Assignment 37

CHAPTER FOUR Breaking Free 39
  Ego: a Major Obstacle to Discovering
  Meaning In Your Life.. 39
  A Personal Encounter With Ego 44
  From Singularity to Unity: Releasing
  the Specter of Ego.. 45
  Who Are You? Perception Is Reality 47
  From External Reality to Internal Truth 49
  Meaning and Perception... 51
  Escaping the Emotional Roller Coaster.................... 52
  Your Fulfilling Life Action Assignment..................... 53

CHAPTER FIVE Discovering Your Worthy Ideal 55
  The Three Devils You Must Avoid:
  Ignorance, Disbelief, and Fear.................................. 55
  Decision is Power... 59
  How to Get What You Really Want 60
  What It Means to Decide 62
  It's Never Too Late to Decide 63
  Imagine That 64
  Small is the Gate and Narrow the Road................... 65
  Your Fulfilling Life Action Assignment..................... 68

CHAPTER SIX Your Quantum Leap............................. 69
  Responsibility and Reciprocity 69
  The Most Influential Aspect of Spiritual Growth 71
  Right-Thinking 73
  A Wormhole to Every Dream 74
  Your Fulfilling Life Action Assignment..................... 76

CHAPTER SEVEN The Nature of Spirit 79
  Defining the Indefinable... 79

Spirit as Principle 82
Spirit as Unity 85
Conversation With a Photon.. 93
Spirit as Love... 94
Your Fulfilling Life Action Assignment.................................. 102

CHAPTER EIGHT The Most Important Question—Ever!.. 105
Personal Gods 108
Interpreting Truth... 110
The Purpose of Corporeal Life 112
The Problem of Knowing and Believing................................ 113
Your Fulfilling Life Action Assignment.................................. 115

CHAPTER NINE Faith and Fear as Creative and Destructive Forces 117
Placebos and Nocebos... 117
Cosmic Power: Your Creative Raw Material 120
According to Your Faith 121
The Power of F.A.I.T.H. 122
Developing Faith.. 127
Making the Quantum Leap 131
Your Fulfilling Life Action Assignment.................................. 134

CHAPTER TEN The Laws of Creation 135
The Process of Creation 135
How Your Thoughts Cause Outcomes 136
The Attractive Force.. 137
The Repulsive Force.. 140
The Polar Forces 141
The Karmic Force 142
Putting the Cart Before the Horse 143

Readjusting the Horse and Cart 145
A Harmonious Arrangement 146
Your Fulfilling Life Action Assignment 147
CHAPTER ELEVEN neuro·ADAPT·ive Programming—
Preparation 149
   Embrace the Power 149
   Perfection Is Not Required 151
   Introduction to neuro·ADAPT·ive Programming 152
   How to Use neuro·ADAPT·ive Programming 155
   There Goes the Baby With the Bathwater 155
   Designing Your Lifestyle 157
   Your Automatic Guidance System 159
   Choosing Your Vehicle 161
   Your Fulfilling Life Action Assignment 162
CHAPTER TWELVE neuro·ADAPT·ive Programming—
Practice 163
   Implementing neuro·ADAPT·ive Programming 163
   Applying the Laws of Creation 163
   Practices to Manage Causes 165
   The Value of Spiritual Practices 171
   The Nine Acts of neuro·ADAPT·ive Programming ... 174
   So, What Now? 182
   Your Fulfilling Life Action Assignment 183
Summary 185

Experiencing Existence Versus Living Life

> "It is not the critic who counts; not the man who points out how the strong man stumbles, or where the doer of deeds could have done them better. The credit belongs to the man who is actually in the arena, whose face is marred by dust and sweat and blood; who strives valiantly; who errs, who comes short again and again, because there is no effort without error and shortcoming; but who does actually strive to do the deeds; who knows great enthusiasms, the great devotions; who spends himself in a worthy cause; who at the best knows in the end the triumph of high achievement, and who at the worst, if he fails, at least fails while daring greatly..."
>
> "Far better it is to dare mighty things, to win glorious triumphs, even though checkered by failure, than to rank with those poor spirits who neither enjoy nor suffer much, because they live in the gray twilight that knows not victory nor defeat."
>
> — **Theodore Roosevelt**

Existence may be experienced from the sidelines of the arena, but *life* itself can only be experienced on the battlefield of living. So, choose your field and fight for what you believe in with all your heart, with all your soul, with all your mind, and with all your strength.

CHAPTER ONE

In the Beginning

When I paused to consider how this book came about, I realized it had been years in the making. It started with religion.

I was raised Catholic but rebelled at the age of thirteen from what felt like a way of life that was hell-bent (pardon the pun) on punishment for sins I had committed. At that age, a sin seemed to be just about anything that was good. Though a lapsed Catholic, I had retained a deep belief in God, but without any particular practice.

A devastating business failure and, more poignantly, the reflection that followed, caused me to look for a more satisfying meaning of and purpose to life, rather than just having a good time, earning money, and accumulating assets. So, I began to meditate and practice yoga and tai chi. Eventually, I came to read the work of nineteenth and twentieth century spiritual teachers like Neville Goddard, Thomas Troward, U. S. Andersen, and Joel Goldsmith, among others. While each had his own unique perspective on the question of existence, they also all agreed that the nature of our consciousness determines the circumstances of our lives. Each also agreed that we can develop our consciousness so that whatever negative influences we subconsciously harbor, like guilt, shame, and anger, may be overcome consciously to better our circumstances. The effect was like a lightbulb coming on in a dark room. Suddenly, everything that I could only previously feel in the room had become visible.

A Universal Problem

When turning from my personal reflections to the world at large, it didn't require any genius on my part to recognize that billions of others around the world were also habitually touched by feelings of unhappiness, insignificance, and aimlessness. Like me, those billions would move quickly between ups and downs, with no apparent way to experience sustained periods of joy. Their happiness or unhappiness would depend on whether external circumstances were favorable in any given moment.

The conclusion has to be that even though each of us is capable of creating our personal circumstances, both consciously and on purpose, when observing the race as a whole, it seems that we are in fact more likely to do so unconsciously and by chance, leading to circumstances we do not care for. When we put aside the various dogmas and personal theologies presented by religionists or held by ourselves, and then read sacred texts afresh, we find that most religions allude to our ability (and even responsibility) to create our lives consciously and on purpose.

The United States has had a prolonged run of being one of the wealthiest nations with the greatest freedoms in the world, yet, there is an often-quoted statistic that hasn't changed much since 1955. It is that, at age sixty-five, 95 percent of Americans are either dead, dead broke, still working (because they have to), on government assistance, or reliant on the charity of friends, family, or charitable organizations. The constancy of this statistic is a good indication that few of us will find deliverance from our feelings of unhappiness, insignificance, and aimlessness in the form of financial riches.

This is not just about money. The 2017 United Nations' *World Happiness Report* ranked the United States fourteenth, behind countries whose own wealth and freedoms ranked significantly lower than America's. In fact, the report further shows that happiness in the United States is on a downward trajectory. This trend is not exclusive to the United States; according to the report, other countries that experienced significant increases in gross domestic product, or GDP, experienced equally spectacular declines in happiness. Before you conclude that there must be a negative correlation between wealth and happiness, I ought to disclose that Norway and Denmark, two wealthy nations, ranked one and two in the same report. So, what's *really* going on?

I believe that, rich or poor, citizens of nations the world over are being led down a blind alley of despair. What we all want is a happy and meaningful life lived as we choose. However, because money is the coin of every realm, we fall into the trap of believing that if we could just get our hands on enough of the stuff, all would be well within our little corner of the world. So, we design our lives around acquiring what we believe will be enough to satisfy *our* version of happiness. But "enough" becomes an ever-increasing value, influenced by persistent advertising propaganda, our envy of celebrity lifestyles, and the opinions of authority figures and our peers. Unwittingly, the pursuit of the mighty dollar, the effervescent euro, or whatever the currency, becomes our religion—and the currency itself becomes our god.

The question is, "Are we doomed to living life this way—whichever way it happens to come at us?" I do not believe so.

The Memories Controlling Your Life

You weren't born with a "Life: 101" manual, so you might not know what you want—and when you do, there'll be times you don't know how to get it.

When you don't know what you want, or how to get it, the result is usually a dead end. A dead-end job. A dead-end relationship. A dead-end struggle for happiness... When coming to a dead end, you'll often make changes based on how you feel about your experiences along the way. Needless to say, when judging an experience as positive, it arouses pleasure and you then want more of the same experience. Conversely, when judging an experience as negative, it causes pain and you subsequently aim to avoid similar experiences.

As a matter of convenience, your feelings about your experiences are stored in your subconscious memory for easy access the next time you encounter similar circumstances. These feelings in turn create automatic responses to new, but similar circumstances. While this sounds like an efficient and convenient way to live, it isn't always the way to a fulfilling life. These stored feelings may serve as a terrific early warning system for avoiding dark alleys in bad neighborhoods, but they may equally prevent you from taking more worthwhile risks like trusting in a romantic relationship or pursuing a potentially life-changing dream you've had since childhood.

The conclusion is that living this way will ensure that you forever react to the external conditions of your life, without ever learning how to proactively overcome them.

The insanity of this kind of life is that it has you trying to manipulate circumstances. Circumstances are, by definition, effects—situations that already exist. Trying to manipulate circumstances—continually trying to repair fatally broken relationships, for example, or attempting to rescue a failing business—will not work until you understand how they came about. Your conveniently stored memories ensure that your life is unconsciously controlled by your subconscious mind. For each stimulus, your subconscious provides an automatic response. Until you accept that your circumstances are the combined effects of how you think and the choices you make that flow naturally from that thought process, you'll be led blindly down the same dead ends, time and again.

The good news is that your subconscious mind is malleable. You can trick it into accepting as reality a circumstance that currently isn't. What can convince your subconscious mind to release its grip on any given belief? Your conscious mind. To change your circumstances, you must develop your consciousness (a term that encompasses both the conscious and subconscious aspects of mind). Developing your consciousness allows your spirit to come through and positively affect your mind. The effects of doing so are expressed in your bodily realm as improved circumstances.

Freedom isn't Free

Developing your consciousness comes at a price, but the return on your investment can be substantial. To reap the rewards, you must first understand how you function.

Each human being is a self-governing system. The human constitution consists of three parts: mind, spirit, and body. We may liken this constitution to that of the

United States, which has three branches of government: legislature, judiciary, and executive. The system works well when there is a separation of powers between each branch for creating, interpreting, and enforcing the constitution. However, mayhem ensues when the powers between branches are ambiguous, so that one branch exercises the powers of another.

With the human constitution, the mind is the legislature, the spirit is the judiciary, and the body the executive branch. However, instead of dealing with constitutional law, the human constitution deals with constitutional decisions. The mind is responsible for creating decisions, the spirit for interpreting those decisions, and the body for executing those decisions. Remember, this system is supposed to be self-governing, but, external influences like what other people think, the brainwashing of advertisers, and the lifestyles of people we admire, may cause us to abdicate our responsibility for self-government. When under the influence of these external stimuli, the separation of decision-making powers becomes ambiguous. A particular problem that arises is that your mind makes decisions that are unconstitutional—contrary to what has been programmed into your subconscious mind.

If the spirit branch interprets the mind's decisions to be unconstitutional, it will judge against the mind. When this happens, all your body's efforts to execute the mind's decisions (which form your goals) will be frustrated and end in failure. You will then be faced with two possibilities: your mind can make decisions that are consistent with what is written in the constitution (i.e., programmed into your subconscious mind), or you can rewrite the constitution itself. In the case of the former, you will get more of what you've been getting. If that is not what you want, you must rewrite the constitution. To do so is to reprogram your subconscious mind.

This idea applies as much to organizations as it does to individuals. The spirit (or soul) of an organization is evidenced by its culture, which is the silent judiciary presiding over how it's supposed to behave. Ideas (legislative function) and behavior (executive function) which are contrary to the cultural norm are generally disapproved of, even when being overtly encouraged by those who set the cultural tone.

Creativity tends to be stifled when the culture condemns failure, and this will be the case regardless of how many creativity initiatives management dreams up. Career progression in such organizations is earned by not upsetting the prevailing state of affairs, and by making the fewest mistakes. Conservatism tends to be a guiding principle—and innovation not.

When the culture embraces failure as a (sometimes) inevitable step toward success, creativity abounds, and ideas are contributed and considered regardless of their source. Career progression tends to be determined more by contribution than by conformity.

When an individual's ideas or behaviors are judged to be unconstitutional (contrary to the culture), that individual has the same two possibilities we considered above: to conform to the norms of the existing constitution, or to challenge it and get a redraft. However, the latter is more difficult to achieve in a conservative organization than in a creative organization, since challenging the existing state of affairs is not part of the conservative culture. A choice to challenge the judiciary in a conservative organization is often synonymous with a decision to leave and go elsewhere.

Two Personal Revelations

Two unconnected personal revelations became the unlikely catalysts for my developing a proprietary creation process called neuro·ADAPT·ive Programming, which enables you to purposely develop the necessary consciousness to create your own fulfilling life. Understanding and consistently applying neuro·ADAPT·ive Programming (along with the other material in the subsequent chapters of this book) is the price of freedom.

The common denominator for my personal revelations was a mind so relaxed that subconscious inspiration was permitted to surface for conscious understanding and use. Since its creation, neuro·ADAPT·ive Programming has been used by coaching clients, and by myself, to significantly improve the circumstances of our lives.

While I was buying groceries in 2015, the only available shopping cart remaining in a busy store had a wobbly wheel (don't you just hate that?) Steering it was so difficult that I almost crashed into another shopper. In a moment of annoyance, I vowed to find a solution to the vexing problem of the wobbly-wheeled shopping cart, the world over. I unsuccessfully played around with various ideas and sketches for months.

One day, I spent so many hours working on the problem that, during meditation that evening, the solution surfaced from my subconscious and into my conscious mind. Instead of a wheel caster, what was required was a ball caster in which the ball rolled smoothly along a set of bearings. This had applications far beyond shopping carts: industrial shelving, wheelbarrows, tables, chairs, and so on.

Once my conscious mind had stopped struggling with the problem, my subconscious mind was able to take over and provide a perfect solution. At the time of writing, the idea is at the prototype phase of development.

Many years before receiving the ball-bearing caster solution, I had a nightmare while overnighting in an unfamiliar city. It was so bad that I went for a run at three in the morning to shake it from my mind. However, once my running stride settled into autopilot, my mind followed suit and started screaming, "THIS IS A CHILDREN'S BOOK!" At first, I couldn't see how. I'd never written a children's book and, until then, had had no thoughts of ever wanting to do so. Most importantly, how could this terrible nightmare be the right material for a children's book anyway?

It's almost anticlimactic to reveal that the entire manuscript for my one and only children's book, *Joshua's Journey: The Life-Changing Flying Adventures of a Minor*, surfaced from the recesses of my subconscious mind during the approximately thirty minutes that remained of my run. The gory, blood-and-guts details of a plane-crash nightmare morphed into a beautiful moral tale, teaching children about wholesome values, everyday courage, everlasting hope, and doing the right thing simply because it's the right thing to do. It was published in 2006, shortly after the nightmare.

These two subconscious revelations inspired me to find a way to produce desired outcomes consciously, consistently, and on demand. And so, neuro·ADAPT·ive Programming was born.

CHAPTER TWO

A New Beginning

What is neuro·ADAPT·ive Programming?

Neuro·ADAPT·ive Programming is a nine-step process that creates change within us and that, in turn, must create change without. As within, so without.

The components of the term neuro·ADAPT·ive Programming have been carefully chosen to precisely define its meaning.

neuro: While the process primarily involves tapping into your subconscious mind (in a very specific way) by using imagination, it is the neurological (or nervous) system that provides the interface between your subconscious and conscious minds. Evidence for this interface is seen in neuroscience, which deals with the structure or function of the nervous system and brain. In particular, we know that imaginations that are vividly experienced can change the brain's neural pathways and synapses, pruning connections that are no longer useful, and creating and strengthening ones that are. This collective neural activity is called neuroplasticity.

ADAPT: This acronym stands for Author, Director, Actor, Producer, and Theater. These are the imaginary characters used in performing the process—*performing* being the operative word. The process involves splitting your mind into the four characters of author, director, actor, and producer, who create and enact a play of your ideal life as an impression upon the theater of your subconscious mind. I am indebted to the late Neville Goddard for these characterizations.

ive: This is another acronym—imagination vividly experienced. The importance of adding emotion and feeling to your play cannot be overstated. This is because emotions are the conduit along which beliefs are transmitted to the subconscious mind.

Programming: The most accurate description of what you are doing to yourself, and for your successful outcome when using the process, is *programming*. With this programming technique, you can create with intention your worthy ideal, your own fulfilling life.

Why Does neuro·ADAPT·ive Programming Work?

Here are five reasons.

1. Your subconscious mind cannot distinguish between what you imagine (particularly with intense emotion) and what is real. One way to demonstrate this point is to close your eyes while holding an imaginary lemon in place on a chopping board. Next, imagine cutting the lemon in half and squeezing its juice into your mouth. Your salivating from this mental exercise is an involuntary act provoked by your subconscious mind assuming you are really squeezing the juice into your mouth. If you don't salivate while doing this exercise, my guess is that you've never experienced the acidity of pure lemon juice.

Creating a Fulfilling Life Through Spiritual Growth 25

2. It is said that a picture is worth a thousand words, and so it would seem. Human thought is experienced either visually or verbally. The former most often occurs when thinking about something like a place, while the latter manifests itself when thinking about something like a report you're going to write. However, a 2017 study by Harvard scientists which was published in the journal *NeuroImage* reveals that visual thinking often intrudes on our verbal thinking. The study concludes that this suggests that visual thinking is more deeply ingrained in the psyche than the more recent evolutionary development of speech. With that being the case, the subconscious mind is more susceptible to influence from pictures than words.

   Furthermore, our lives are lived in motion. So, creating a motion picture for your subconscious mind to feed on increases the chances of it accepting the picture as real.

3. Thoughts, feelings, attitudes, and memories, once stored in your subconscious mind, unconsciously govern your behaviors. An obvious example occurs most days you drive your car, particularly along familiar routes. You can be consciously thinking of other things while you speed along on autopilot. This unconscious competence was developed by practicing the skill of driving over time. Repeatedly feeding your subconscious mind material which is consistent with your ideal fulfilling life by using neuro·ADAPT·ive Programming, has the same effect; it reprograms the subconscious to prevent the *default* stored material from producing results you don't want, and to promote this new material producing the results you *do* want.

4. This new material—thoughts, feelings, attitudes, and memories—creates the experiences you want by the law of attraction.

5. The human inclination for naming things isn't a chance occurrence; it is a necessity of this stage in human evolution, an inseparable part of our intellectual capacity. Not being able to put names to numbers, for example, would make them more difficult to conceptualize and extremely difficult to share with others. Naming a thing (even if only mentally) reinforces the concept of it. To say that it makes the concept more concrete is fitting; naming it is a step in the process of creating it. Biblically, "The word becomes flesh"—material (John 1:1). Using the worthy ideal statement that you'll develop in chapter 4, together with the sensualization technique from the nine acts of neuro·ADAPT·ive Programming in chapter 12, will help you to advance your fulfilling life from dream to reality.

So, What is a Fulfilling Life, Anyway?

If you take a close look at individuals you regard as truly successful, you'll notice that they do not necessarily have great jobs, pursue rewarding careers, or have amazing businesses. Instead, what you'll notice is that they are on a mission to serve; and by serving a lot, they receive a lot. Despite some of them having a lot of money, and other outward suggestions of success, the thread of commonality running through them all is the possession of a desire to fulfill a purpose expressed by their mission. What they earn is merely a byproduct of what they love doing, the latter providing more than money ever can—a rich, deep meaning and satisfaction that becomes commonplace in their lives.

If asked to choose one or the other, I cannot imagine either Bill Gates or the late Steve Jobs choosing their financial wealth over the virtuous wealth which they created through improving the world for humankind forever. I'm equally certain that neither Gandhi nor Mother Teresa would have swapped the virtuous wealth they created for any amount of financial wealth. By virtuous wealth, I mean the experiences they endured and those they enjoyed from doing what they did, and their satisfaction in becoming who they were from serving the world as they did.

With this in mind, I encourage you to design your ideal lifestyle around a worthy ideal you strongly identify with and strongly believe in, without any consideration for financial gain. I'm not asking you to become a pauper; just to reposition what's most important for long-term success, which is peace of mind gained from living a deeply fulfilling life.

The global population is approaching 8 billion. Presupposing an omniscient Creator, I have to imagine that if It could carry out Its grand plan with just 8 people, It would do so. I would also have to imagine that each of the nearly 8 billion (and counting) must have a unique role to play, no matter how great or slight the differences.

Your Life is Like a Pendulum

Each person's life can be likened to a pendulum. For the purpose of this comparison, let's suppose that the pendulum's ideal fulfilling life is achieved when it is at rest—perpendicular to the earth's surface. While at rest, it appears to be idle, but in fact, it's not. The force which positively influences the attainment of its fulfilling life purpose, is gravity. Gravity unceasingly pulls the pendulum vertically toward the center of the earth, and so is in alignment with the pendulum's own ideal. Because the force and the ideal are in alignment, the pendulum only *appears* to be idle. A better adjective for the pendulum's apparent idleness is *ease*. The pendulum is at ease.

Sadly for the pendulum, gravity is not the only force acting upon it. There are interfering individuals who want to pull it this way and that for their own amusement. The pendulum swings from side to side under the influence of the sideways momentum created by the interfering individuals. Despite this interference however, the weight of the pendulum's ideal is so strong that, little by little, it purposely gets back on track toward its fulfilling life with the aid of its supportive force—gravity.

Like the pendulum, a fulfilling life is one built around an ideal that is your own. It doesn't have to be grand; with so many people at Its disposal, the Creator does not require the majority to be celebrity movie stars, renowned rocket scientists, or serial inventors. It is outstanding to be a tinker, tailor, soldier, or sailor if being one of these is what your soul yearns for you to be. In my experience working with many people, I've come to learn that a fulfilling life is one that has an ideal bigger than yourself, which is focused on serving others.

The problem is that, like the pendulum, we too are pulled from side to side by generic societal ideas of what a fulfilling life is: a trophy spouse, $10 million in the bank, straight white teeth, celebrity status, and never failing at anything, to name a few components thereof. While the pendulum has only one counterforce to deal with (side-to-side momentum), we also have to overcome burdensome societal norms, the lure of seemingly greener pastures, potentially exciting, though distracting experiences, our own apathy, and our own fears. To get back on track, we need a force so strong, like the pendulum's gravity, that it brings us back to our original purpose. That force is what I call a worthy ideal statement. This is not simply something that you chant as a mantra, but is also a way of being—a state of consciousness.

When you are in the flow of living your meaningful life on purpose, it can be more active and yet less stressful. You are more at ease, though not idle. There is work to be done, and *you* love doing it.

Your Roadmap

The rest of this book is about the psychological and spiritual development required to purposely create your fulfilling life. Chapters 3 through 10 lay the groundwork for using neuro·ADAPT·ive Programming; they discuss why we need to live life not just as mind and body, but also as spirit. Finally, Chapters 11 and 12 bring to bear what has been learned in the previous chapters with an explanation of how you can use neuro·ADAPT·ive Programming to create your own fulfilling life on purpose. Each of the remaining chapters also includes a Fulfilling Life Action Assignment based on material in each respective chapter. These have been carefully crafted to aid the purposeful creation of your fulfilling life.

Some Assertions About Being Human

When living principally from the perspective of body, we are dominated by our bodily needs; responding to physiological urges for food, sex, shelter, and warmth, above all else. Satisfying these needs is pleasurable, while not doing so is painful. From the perspective of body, our main concern is the instant gratification of its needs. The taste of food is more important than its nutritional value, sexual stimulation is more important than a relationship, and so on.

> **When living principally from the perspective of body, we are dominated by our bodily needs; responding to physiological urges for food, sex, shelter, and warmth, above all else.**

When biased toward living from the perspective of mind, we are preoccupied with appearances. Our main aim is to fit in, so we indiscriminately adopt societal norms and values without much consideration for what they might mean for our uniqueness. While keeping up with the Joneses, the real "us" is consumed by the identity of the social group, be it family, political party, workplace, or nation.

Your spiritual self is immaterial. To experience it, you must still your body and silence your mind. When persistent aspirants discern the divine within, their desire to be their unique selves surfaces and, at last, they find the resources to create fulfilling lives around their unique worthy ideals that are consumed with their passion.

It is difficult to speak of these three facets of human being without a sense of progressive development from body to mind, and on to spirit. This is a misconception. Each is important in its own right, and inseparable from the whole being. Remove any one of the facets of legs, seat, or back from a chair and it ceases to be a chair. A human being that does not have all of body, mind, and spirit is not a human being.

However, if we do regard the evolution of our lives as a progressive development from body to mind, then on to spirit, such progression must end in our effective disembodiment and consequent ineffectiveness in the world. When we truly understand our spirituality, we recognize that our collective bodies are the Creator's hands, so to speak, and our collective minds, the Creator's mind. It is through humanity's collective body and mind that the higher levels of material evolution are possible. We don't perceive the Creator *and* humanity, but that humanity *is* the Creator, manifested in bodily form. While I will continue to refer to this unfathomable part of humanity as the Creator throughout the rest of this book, it is arguable from the foregoing, that the most fitting name for It is the Higher Self.

Spiritual development, then, is not an evolution beyond body and mind, to spirit. It is the three parts progressing simultaneously, as one.

A friend once said to me, "You know, Lennox, I've just realized that all of my years studying personal development material have been little more than entertainment." To my response of, "How do you mean?" he replied, "I've never really followed through with the actions required to obtain the benefits from the material." This is a book about creating a fulfilling life. Creation requires action. By completing the action assignments at the end of each chapter, you'll get the maximum benefit from this book.

It is my sincere wish that you don't just read this book, but that you apply and share its principles with others. Creating a fulfilling life on purpose must involve making a contribution to improve the lives of others. Therefore, the greatest reward I can receive for writing this book is to hear from you about how you are writing, producing, directing, and starring in your own blockbuster, fulfilling a life that is rich with your personality and created on your terms. You can contact me via my website: www.lennoxcornwall.com.

CHAPTER THREE

Existing on Autopilot

What I'm about to share here may not be your factual reality in particular, but it is likely to be your metaphorical truth; and, unless it's understood and taken to heart, you'll never become the person you yearn to be.

Thank You, I've Got This

The inclination to exist on autopilot begins at birth. And, *this* is how it began for you...

You were born. You needed to start breathing oxygen under the steam of your own lungs, so the midwife smacked you on the bum. Right then and there, you had to make your first decision: to cry or to say, "Thank you, sister. I've got this. I'll take it from here!" The former decision would lead to forming limiting beliefs, the latter to forming empowering beliefs.

For the sake of transparency, I want you to know that my mom told me I cried; therefore, I can say that your first breath is not the only chance you'll get to make something of life. Opportunities to do so can be found in the many trials that lie ahead. With each one you'll be faced with the same decision: to adopt a crying posture or one that says to life, "Thank you for the lesson. I've got this. I'll take it from here!"

The cumulative effects of the decisions you make—both cowardly and brave—determine your success. When a person's decisions are mainly based on negotiating the path of least resistance and experiencing the least amount of pain while doing so, they'll likely end up in a rut disguised as a comfort zone. There are times when life can be tough. Sometimes, you just want to escape from the responsibility to grow and be your best self. There are many diversions that provide the relief you're looking for. Karl Marx referred to religion as the opium of the people, and this can be the case if it is used to abdicate personal responsibility for your growth. The same can be true of overindulgence in social media, excessive fantasy sports league participation, overworking, not working, living vicariously through your children, social drinking, and so on, if such activities are used as escapes from the trials and tribulations involved in the pursuit of emotional, psychological, and spiritual maturity.

The Most Dangerous Hidden Trap

As the name suggests, the comfort zone presents an appearance of comfort; a psychologically warm, cozy place to take a rest from the hardships of pressing on with life. Of course, this is indeed the case; however, like your warm, cozy bed in the middle of winter, you mustn't rest too long. There's work to be done.

When you pause from your routine, you may recognize the rut you're in. Despite this, you are in danger of dusting yourself off and carrying on as if nothing has happened (to paraphrase Sir Winston Churchill speaking about what some of us do when we discover truth). Resisting change that would better your life is like growing a fruit tree you hope will bear the juiciest fruit come harvest time, then refusing to prune it.

Each time life smacks you on the bum, your perception of the world is either reinforced or shifted. A reinforcement has you more firmly stuck in your comfort zone, whereas a shift causes you to move forward or backward. For example, the loss of a loved one could cause one person to see life as more hopeless and fated, while for another, it could be the catalyst that helps them live life to the fullest.

It's worth repeating that a crying posture creates limiting beliefs, while deciding to "take it from here!" creates empowering beliefs. If you believe that money is hard to come by, you'll find it hard to come by; if you believe that success is difficult, you will find it to be difficult; if you believe that you are a poor communicator, you will be. Your life is a self-fulfilling prophesy, and YOU are the prophet—but not one that reads the future; one that creates it! It has been said that the subconscious mind knows only one word: "yes!" So, every time you really believe something to be your reality—true or not—your subconscious will effectively say, "Thanks for sharing. I've got this. I'll take it from here," and deliver that reality.

Escape Is Close at Hand

Escaping the autopilot lifestyle requires a psychological movement beyond the interplay of pain and pleasure, and beyond the stimulus-response mechanism that even the single-celled amoeba is fully equipped to deal with. Surely, as the pinnacle of the Creator's finest work, more is expected of humanity. Unlike amoebas, we can ascribe meaning to our lives. Doing so is how we find the answers to triumphantly escape the stagnation of the comfort zone and move onward to fulfillment.

> *Your life is a self-fulfilling prophesy, and YOU are the prophet—but not one that reads the future; one that creates it!*

> *"Man's main concern is not to gain pleasure or to avoid pain but rather to see a meaning in his life."*
>
> —Viktor Frankl

We are destined to remain trapped in the comfort zone until we ascribe meaning to our lives that is more compelling than the status quo. Any such meaning must elevate us beyond the trivia that we allow to dominate our lives. Examples of trivial or trite meaning that we may ascribe to our lives can include feeling especially learned, acclaiming great taste in wines, boasting about knowing so-and-so personally, having pretensions about being voted chair of the homeowners' association for three consecutive terms, or being prideful about earning a particular level of income. There is nothing wrong with any of these when they are embraced with a perspective commensurate with their importance. Too often, however, we elevate their significance to fill the void which has been created in the absence of a deeper meaning to our lives. Chapter 4 marks the beginning of our quest to find that deeper meaning.

Your Fulfilling Life Action Assignment

It is easy to become sidetracked by the many distractions forced on us by family, friends, media outlets, and marketers. Remaining focused is made even more difficult when accounting for the modern-day "necessity" to be in constant contact with the wider world. We are unwittingly sidetracked by incessant texting and nonstop engagement with social media platforms—Facebook, Twitter, Snapchat, Instagram, YouTube, and so on. The tendency for these to become *weapons of mass distraction* calls for sincere discrimination in their use, if you are serious about attaining a life blessed with fulfillment.

Remember, the cumulative effects of the decisions you make—both cowardly and brave—determine your success. With this in mind, how can you change the way you interact with the wider world to ensure that the interaction is helping rather than hindering the attainment of your fulfilling life?

CHAPTER FOUR

Breaking Free

Ego: a Major Obstacle to Discovering Meaning In Your Life

Ego is perhaps the most significant obstacle to discovering a profoundly worthy meaning for your life.

The celebrated psychologist Carl Jung saw the ego as the center of our consciousness—a place where our sense of identity resides. It is difficult to accurately define what that really means. I believe that ego comes from a combination of experiences stored in the mind as self-perceptions—like self-esteem, self-worth, and self-image—that are then expressed behaviorally as emotions—like arrogance, pride, and pretense. Together, these perceptions and emotions form a protective shell around your personality, preventing others from seeing you as you truly are, and preventing you from seeing the world as it truly is. The late spiritual teacher U. S. Andersen said that ego "...has us believing that we are greater than others, and less than we truly are."

Ego can con you into going through life thinking that you're special, while not knowing that you're unique. There is nothing special about your left foot compared

> *Ego can con you into going through life thinking that you're special, while not knowing that you're unique.*

with your right hand, but each is certainly unique. Likewise, you are not special, but one in the unified amalgam of humanity; and yet, you are unique. No matter how many trillions of persons come before and after, there will only ever be one you.

None of this is to say that ego is bad. Ego is the psychological eggshell that protects your self-image. Without its protection, your self-image in your formative years, when exposed to more mature personalities, would suffer the imposition of those personalities on your own fledgling personality. Indeed, even with the ego's protection this can happen, especially with children and usually from well-meaning, or at least impartial, guardians and peers.

One of your greatest challenges is to achieve an incredible balancing act between protecting your self-identity (self-image) from ego, while preventing ego from restricting your psychological and spiritual growth. Figuratively, a chick achieves this by cracking its eggshell. However, the cracking of your psychological eggshell—ego—could be detrimental, leaving you exposed to the directives of everyone else. The risk is a loss of self-identity that results in you assuming the identity—good or bad—given to you by others. We sometimes see such a cracking of the ego in persons who have suffered loss through divorce, death, job redundancy, business failure, empty-nest syndrome, or anything else that may negatively impact their self-identity.

Rather than cracking your ego shell, what is required is its stretching to accommodate your spiritual liberation. As you grow spiritually, your psyche becomes more resilient to the emotional blows that you will inevitably encounter in life. As the psyche becomes more resilient, the shell's protective wall stretches and becomes thinner and thinner to the point of vanishing completely (should you achieve enlightenment). This, of course, is a figurative description of the challenge I am outlining: to achieve a balance between protecting your self-identity from ego while preventing ego from restricting your psychological and spiritual growth. With spiritual growth, you are able to enjoy the richness of corporeal life—relationships, business endeavors, health, etc.—without the debilitating effects of separation caused by perceived loss.

How can this spiritual growth be achieved? The practices provided in chapter 12, together with three principles found in many world religions—not resisting evil, turning the other cheek, and praying for your enemies—provide a solid foundation for growth. Adopting these three principles does not mean you should allow or encourage others to treat you badly. By the law of attraction, what you focus on expands in your life in proportion to the attention you give to it.

By not resisting the evils of someone spreading gossip about you, stabbing you in the back at work, or criticizing your political or religious beliefs, you restrict the negative effects of those evils in your life. Sure, you should represent your true position on these matters, but don't disrespect your opponent's position. This is contrary to what we see in public life. It seems that to win a political campaign, for instance, requires being economical with the truth and running smear campaigns against your opponents. In our private lives, however, we find much more success taking the opposite approach.

Treat this as social *aikido*—the way of the harmonious spirit. Morihei Ueshiba developed the Japanese martial art of aikido so that practitioners could protect themselves from attackers, while also protecting the attackers themselves from injury. Practitioners learn to flow with the force of an attacker rather than resisting it head on.

Aikido's techniques are described as so gentle that even the attacker is delighted. "Delighted" is how I pray you leave your persecutors. Just as with the martial art, social aikido is more about victory over yourself than victory over your opponents.

The most common interpretation of turning the other cheek is to allow others to abuse you more than they already have. However, it is said of the one who encouraged us to do so that he spoke to the masses in parables, or not at all. Therefore, a more beneficial interpretation of turning the other cheek is as a figure of speech, encouraging us to turn our attention away from what we don't want and onto what we do. Let me show you what I mean, using a mental exercise. Imagine that you are slapped on the right cheek; the blow would turn your head to the left. So, looking at the world from your left side is the perspective you gain along with the pain of the blow. Now, turn your head to the right. Immediately you have a different view—a different perspective. A perspective without the pain of the blow.

To pray for your enemies is to genuinely intend the best for them. The section on spirit as love in chapter 7 shows why this may not be as difficult for you as you might assume. For now, it's enough to say that when you perceive the unity of all things, inflicting injury on others through thought, word, or deed becomes distasteful. You will know that to do so is to injure yourself because all that exists is immersed in the singular universal consciousness. While you may not notice it directly, injuring another is like releasing a toxic gas into the air around them. Eventually that gas will come back to hurt you, since you are breathing the same air. Praying for an enemy, on the other hand, is like releasing a delightful fragrance into the air around them. You, too, will be touched by the effects of this fragrance. With this new perspective, loving your neighbors and praying for your enemies should no longer be a commandment to obey, but a necessity for well-being, like breathing air.

A Personal Encounter With Ego

Breaking free of ego's grip is a difficult business. It involves adopting new values and reacting differently to what may seem natural, like retaliating against criticism. The path of progress is unlikely to be upwardly smooth, and more likely to resemble the upward trajectory of a volatile stock price.

Some years ago, in a former career, I created a sales presentation that significantly increased my closing ratio with prospective clients. It was so effective that the national sales director publicly congratulated me for my ingenuity and wanted to roll out the presentation to the entire salesforce. In the meantime, I was asked to train a new-hire sales manager for another sales channel the company had recently started. I shared my presentation with the new guy, who achieved a lot of success with it. Before long, my presentation became the new guy's idea. The same national sales director who had publicly congratulated me for the idea (before the new guy was even hired) also attributed my idea to the new guy. How could this be? I was enraged, outraged, and *in* a rage! My relationships with the national sales director, the new guy, and other coworkers deteriorated because of my sense of injustice.

If you have a heart, you'll feel my pain. If you've grasped the power inherent in adopting the above-mentioned three principles, you'll see through my pain. My behavior was completely egocentric—it was all about me. In hindsight, I realize that the senior management's desire for the new sales channel to succeed was so great that they were prepared to demonstrate its success by (unjustly) attributing my idea to a manager in that new channel. They, like I, are full of human imperfections. Knowing this about humanity, we may expect the best of people and, yet, not be devastated by their worst. If I had had the wisdom for discovering the meaning of my life back then, my manager's offense would have had me turning the other cheek, praying for him, and not resisting what I had perceived as evil.

From Singularity to Unity: Releasing the Specter of Ego

The concurrence of greater resilience to emotional trauma and an increasingly thinner ego shell culminates in enlightenment, which is the absence of ego and complete resilience to emotional trauma. Jungian psychology refers to this as ego collapse. This resilience should not be confused with hard-heartedness; an enlightened person is one who has acquired the attributes of spirit—love, forgiveness, gratitude, joy—as completely as is possible in corporeal life. The enlightened are able to fully absorb these attributes mentally and so fully express them physically. It is a state in which body, mind, and spirit are in perfect harmony. In this enlightened state (and by the law of attraction), you are not touched by the ills of the world, since what you attract to yourself is of a kind that is comparable to what you already are. The conversation in chapter 9 on converting cosmic power to personal power demonstrates how this harmonization of the three realms of human being is achieved, in order to improve your effectiveness in every area of life.

Most do not achieve this state of enlightenment. So,

what then? In this lower state of consciousness, we want to be like everyone else, so do whatever we can to fit in. The desire to fit in can be so strong that we are prepared to take sometimes immoral, and even illegal measures to do so. Most often, the goal is avoiding such social censorship as may occur when not compromising within the family, when failing in business, when uneager to please another in a relationship, or when threatened with job loss by seeming at odds with the workplace culture.

While socially acceptable, the goal to fit in may conflict with discovering a deeper meaning of life and attaining a greater fulfillment therein. You remain in the comfort zone, potentially exposed to living a life of quiet desperation. The desperation of wanting to be more, but not knowing what "more" is, causes us to imitate what others have done: acquire more possessions, fall into another relationship, change jobs, have another child, and so on. With each new situation, we strive to fill an unidentified emptiness within. What we miss is that the people we are emulating don't know what "more" is either. Ultimately, "more" is a more meaningful life with greater fulfillment, only we don't know how to achieve and express that. The sad irony is that no one ever gets a more meaningful life by playing it safe in the comfort zone. You have to risk being your true self—standing out from the crowd and facing social censorship for doing so, if necessary—to have a meaningful life. Let me give you an example of this.

Many years ago, I had a friend who was a renowned cardiologist in London. He had all the so-called trappings of success: an amazing home, a beautiful wife, equally beautiful children with great careers ahead of them, lots of money, the admiration of his colleagues, and so on. You may be thinking, "What's the problem?" The problem was that while he had succeeded greatly as a cardiologist, being one was not actually his idea of a meaningful and fulfilling life but, instead, a dream he had adopted as a child. His parents had convinced him that being a cardiologist would bring him the trappings of success. They hadn't lied; it did. What he didn't realize is the same thing that tens of millions of others don't realize until it is too late. "Trappings" is the operative word in the statement. We literally get trapped on the treadmill known as the Pursuit of Success, but we are then lost to the Pursuit of Happiness. These are not one and the same. If you engage in the former, *without* being true to yourself, you seldom end up with the fruits of the latter. However, pursuing the latter is the most efficient way to achieve both.

As for my friend, he couldn't face the ridicule from family and friends of pursuing his dream. What he wanted was to own a health-food store that would allow him to proactively help prevent the causes of heart disease, instead of reactively treating them. He remained trapped in his comfort zone. His life of quiet desperation caused him severe bouts of anxiety and depression, and a deep sense of loneliness in a crowded home. He was definitely *in need* of comfort.

Who Are You? Perception Is Reality

The continued existence and nature of the ego, beyond its necessity to protect a developing personality, depends on the question, "Who am I?" Your answer may fall somewhere between two positions: the first is feeling like an individual droplet of water in a universe that was created by chance (where your purpose is to compete with others for a living in a hostile environment over which you have no control), while the second is recognizing yourself

> *We literally get trapped on the treadmill known as the Pursuit of Success, but we are then lost to the Pursuit of Happiness.*

as a droplet of water within the unity of the entire ocean of life that has been created with a specific purpose in mind.

The self-image derived from your ego will determine your personality. As the individual droplet of water, you may imagine yourself as being a single competitor in a game called life, in which someone else winning means you losing. Winning is defined in possessing people, experiences, and things. You perceive your ultimate destination as eternal death.

By contrast, as the droplet of water that knows it is a part of the ocean, you understand that you're not special, but a unique expression of the whole ocean. As the ocean crashes against the rocks, you—the droplet—are flung into existence for a brief moment in time, before crashing back into the ocean. When you cease to be a droplet, by this inevitable falling back into the ocean, you realize that your life goes on. Your mantra is, "I and the ocean are one." You are in the ocean and yet the ocean is in you. You recognize your spiritual immortality in unity in spite of your individual mind-body mortality. Chapters 7 and 8 consider in more detail the importance that self-image plays in your ability to discover meaning for your life, and to attain fulfillment from it.

From External Reality to Internal Truth

An enlightened person does not choose one reality over another, but accepts the truth of what is. That truth is found in the stillness at the center of their being.

When your primary experience of life is as body or mind, you use physical measures to dull psychological pain. However, these are counterfeit measures attempting

> *Spiritual growth, then, is the progressive realization of the truth that lies within.*

to change your reality. Generally speaking, this can be seen in comfort eating to relieve boredom, alcohol abuse to mask stress, and overworking to forget loneliness. All these attempts, because they are counterfeit, are short-term solutions and require increasingly stronger and larger doses to relieve whatever it is we are trying to escape.

To experience your life as spirit is to overcome the habit of turning to external resources for strength, comfort, security, peace, and pleasure. By living from within, you find these attributes from within. In turn, because they are sourced from within, they are genuine and unaffected by external circumstances or the fluctuations of mind and emotions. The ego shell thins and who you are inside shines brightly outward. The congruency of the internal with the external is an attractive force that draws good to you.

The process toward congruency is ongoing. You don't have to be a fully-fledged, card-carrying spiritual guru to work toward congruency. The more you become engrossed in your worthy ideal, the weaker the effects of external circumstances are, and your old disserving habits start falling by the wayside. Spiritual growth, then, is the progressive realization of the truth that lies within.

Meaning and Perception

When experiencing life from body or mind, you define (see meaning in) who you are by the material things and the relationships you have. However, there is no meaning in anything physical, whether person, place, or thing. Meaning comes from your perception of a thing. The universe is ever-evolving so, by their nature, all physical things are subject to change: growth, decay, death, etc.

As things change, they no longer match your perception and you will experience pleasure or pain according to whether or not the changes meet the expectations that your perception created.

The parts of you that are body and mind are also subject to change. When they do change, your perceptions of yourself and of others also change, causing more pain or pleasure, discomfort or delight in:

- What your body looks like;
- What other people's bodies look like;
- Your financial state of affairs;
- Your relationships;
- Where you live;
- The work that you do;
- The routines that you keep;

and so on.

A change in your perception is also effectively a change in yourself, and so, who you *are* no longer matches other people's perceptions of who you *were*; They will like you less or more; you and they will experience more pain or pleasure accordingly. No wonder the world can seem to be a hostile, unpredictable place.

Escaping the Emotional Roller Coaster

There is simply no way of escaping this emotional roller coaster while living principally from body or mind, any more than a mouse can escape the limitations of being a mouse by being housed in a mansion in the country instead of a shack in the hood. The only way out is to transcend body and mind to live from within yourself, to live from spirit. In doing so, you realize that "you're in this world, but not of it," by which I mean your true, unchanging self is spiritual, while your body-mind selves are your perceived reality and, therefore, subject to change. The closer your perceived reality matches spiritual truth, the shorter the peaks and troughs of your emotional roller coaster will be. Through this smoothing out, you'll find that you enjoy more prolonged periods of peace, joy, and love. As you grow spiritually, the smoothness becomes even smoother and you become able to realize greater fulfillment from your life.

Your Fulfilling Life Action Assignment

Ego is a protective shell around your personality, preventing others from seeing you as you truly are and preventing you from seeing the world as it truly is. Bad habits are often a way for the ego to protect against changes in personality, which unfortunately restrict your growth.

What is the main bad habit you need to give up in order to achieve the fulfilling life you dream of? For example; binge TV watching or eating, excessive alcohol, over- or underworking, or abusing others or yourself?

Bad habits become characteristic through repetition. Giving up a bad habit can be difficult because we derive psychological satisfaction from customary behaviors. This psychological satisfaction is often reinforced by a physical satisfaction from the release of endorphins when the bad habit is exercised. The two steps you can take to get rid of a bad habit are:

1. Mentally associating the habit with something you really don't like and/or would hate to happen to you.

For instance, with binge TV watching, you could visualize the lifeforce draining out of you while sitting there, absorbed in unproductive behavior; and

2. Replacing the bad habit with a good one. Just as bad habits become characteristic through repetition, so too do good ones. You will also benefit from the same psychological and physical satisfactions. Only now you will be moving toward your fulfilling life.

So, what negative mental association will you make with the bad habit, and what good habit will you replace it with?

CHAPTER FIVE

Discovering Your Worthy Ideal

The Three Devils You Must Avoid: Ignorance, Disbelief, and Fear

There are three destructive forces that prevent you from being, doing, and having what you want. They are ignorance, disbelief, and fear.

Ignorance is total oblivion, like driving your car toward a cliff you don't know is there; disbelief is not believing in something you are aware of; and fear is a belief that something is likely to be dangerous or cause you pain. Although the unpleasant outcome hasn't actually occurred, with fear, you experience the negative effects anyway. So, we can define fear as **F**uture **E**vil **A**lready **R**ealized (when it doesn't have to be), or as the age-old **F**alse **E**vidence **A**ppearing **R**eal. The first definition keeps you stuck, while the second one frees you. Choose one!

There are a litany of dream-stealing ideas and behaviors that spring from the three devils. Here are just a few:

Ignorance

Hate

Misplaced faith

Fatalism

Disbelief

Mistrust

Laziness

Ambivalence

Fear

Procrastination

Indecisiveness

Insecurity

Let's take a look at how just one of these dream-stealing behaviors—indecisiveness—may affect your plans.

Imagine building your dream home. Your basic design and plans are refined and completed by an architect. You select a great builder who gets right to work. Everything is on course and on budget, until...you change your mind about where the garage should be. So, you inform the architect, who redraws the plans and submits them to the builder. You're back on course, until...you realize that a fourth bedroom will be needed. So, you go back and inform the architect, who redraws the plans and submits them to the builder for a third time. Again, you're back on course, until...you have an argument with your ailing mother, who decides she now wants to live with your brother in Florida. You're openly happy about this because you knew your spouse was secretly against the idea anyway. There is now no need for that fourth bedroom or the change in garage placement, since you decided on the latter to please your mother as well. You may as well inform the architect to save some money. The architect redraws the plans to the exact specifications that you began with and submits them to the builder for a fourth time, and you're back on course...finally.

Now, let's imagine that the builder represents your subconscious mind, the architect your conscious mind, and you, your corporeal self. Your dream home in this example could represent any goal that you want to achieve. Every time you issue new instructions, your conscious mind has to impress a new directive upon your subconscious mind, which then has to stop the process of manifesting what you said you wanted, throw out the plans, undo some or all of what has already been done, then start anew. If the time period for the completion of your goal was twelve months, each discontinuation and redirection may add, say, an additional five months. Taking the above case of your dream home as the example, an additional fifteen months have therefore been added to the timeline for completion. There is also the likely significant increase in tangible costs associated with the project, and the intangible opportunity costs of what else you could have achieved with the time and effort that you had to instead devote to each change.

Whenever you find yourself asking, "Why is this goal taking much longer to realize than I expected?" ask yourself the subsequent question, "How committed in thoughts and actions have I been to the goal?" A lack of commitment is often why your goal is delayed or left unfulfilled.

Commitment is doing what you said you'd do long after the mood you said it in has left you.

—George Zalucki, psychologist and entrepreneur

> *A lack of commitment is often why your goal is delayed or left unfulfilled.*

Decision is Power

The importance of making good decisions may be appreciated from the diverse, multi-billion-dollar decision-making marketplace in which the many decision-making tools available include courses, webinars, seminars, coaching, consulting, software programs, hardware, chaos theory, zero-sum game theory, mathematical modeling, bio-computing, predictive index modeling, risk assessment, astrology, numerology, crystal balls, tarot cards, palm reading, tea leaves, and coffee grounds. While success may be preceded by an ambition, it begins with a definite decision to pursue that ambition.

For our purposes, we can ignore all of the tools listed above and focus on the only thing that matters, which is, *what do you really want?* In considering this question, you must ignore what other people want you to be, do, or have. You must ignore their opinions regarding who you are and what you're capable of. A mantra I once created and used to get me past other people's opinions of who I should be, is:

"With my attention focused on who I am, I cannot be distracted by the person others want me to be."

"Other people" may include coworkers and mentors, or your closest family and friends. Continuing to love and respect them does not mean being, doing, or having what they want for you. Until and unless you really start pursuing what you want to be, do, and have, you'll likely never be truly happy or achieve the lasting success found within peace of mind. One of life's great ironies is that many who want to stand out try to do so by being someone else, when the shortcut to standing out is to simply be yourself.

Think about what it is you really want. In doing so,

ignore all the reasons why you can't be it, do it, or have it: I don't have enough money; I don't have enough time; I'm not good enough; I'm too ugly; I don't deserve it; I'm in poor health; I've tried it unsuccessfully before; no one in my family has ever done that before; I wonder what people would think of me if I did that; I have invested so much time and money in my existing career (or business), how could I just leave that all behind?; I have the children to think about; I'm too old; I'm too young; and so on.

Ignore all of these. The countless millions who have overcome similar reasons to realize their worthy ideal could argue that these reasons are really just excuses. However, let's not argue. Rather than personalizing these things as reasons or excuses, let us, instead, objectify them as situations. It doesn't matter so much what you feel about them as what you *do* about them. That is a matter of choice—your choice.

How to Get What You Really Want

One of the biggest challenges to overcoming any of the situations cited is telling whoever will listen, "You don't understand, my situation is different!" People all over the world use this same faulty reasoning while, around and about them, a chosen few (self-chosen, that is) have overcome the very same situation that has others stuck and then gone on to realize their ambitions. Everyone's situation is different and yet similar. If your worthy ideal is worthy of the description "*worthy ideal*," you won't be able to rely on reason alone to achieve it.

> *"The reasonable man adapts himself to the world; the unreasonable one persists in trying to adapt the world to himself. Therefore, all progress depends on the unreasonable man."*
>
> —**George Bernard Shaw**

Let us be clear what we mean by reasonable. In this context, reasonable means staying within the accepted boundaries of common sense. Achieving worthy ideals is not based on reasonable thinking or common sense. I don't want you to think outside the box, or even *be* outside the box. I want you to realize that there *is no box*. It is a figment of an imagination conditioned to limitation.

If I were your personal genie that could grant you your every wish in exchange for your putting in five full days of work, for forty-eight weeks each year, what work would you do? It does not have to be for pay or profit. Genie Lennox will bestow abundance upon every area of your life, regardless.

Now, based on that, write out a specific worthy ideal that you want to achieve. Here are some rules to follow:

1. Make it all about you. Use "I," "I am," or any first-person phrase to begin the statement. In doing this, you are creating a state-*meant*. In other words, you are intentionally developing your consciousness to become who you want to be, do what you want to do, and get what you want to get. As Mahatma Gandhi wisely said, "Be the change you wish to see in the world." You cannot have it unless you become it. What you desire is not out there somewhere, but within you—a state of consciousness.

2. Write it as though you already have it. By doing so, your subconscious mind assumes the state you need to be in to have what you want.

3. Make your statement clear and simple. If an average eight-year-old doesn't understand it, rewrite it until they do, if at all possible.

4. Where possible, make sure the statement has a component describing your service to others as well as stating exactly who you want to be (in the present tense).

Here's an example of what a worthy ideal statement should look like:

"I am an international bestselling author. My work is available through multiple media on a continuous basis and raises the conscious awareness of millions of people around the world."

Once you have your worthy ideal, the next stage is to begin the process of realizing it.

What It Means to Decide

It is accepted wisdom that the pace of change quickens with every age. As such, it should be no surprise that the use and meaning of words can change with changing times; sometimes subtly, and sometimes radically. It is often helpful, therefore, to go back to the origin of a word to get a more precise sense of its meaning.

The origin of *decide* is literally "to cut off." What is being cut off, then, is all other options. There is no exit strategy. That is not to say that there can be no other strategy to achieve your worthy ideal. Hitting your head against a brick wall when the strategy isn't getting you there is insanity—and not a way to achieve your worthy ideal. If the first, second, third, or umpteenth strategy doesn't work, find another one. The point is that alternative strategies are taking you toward your dream—and not the nearest exit.

Interestingly, the meaning of the adjective *decided* is "a reality that is not in doubt." Note, therefore, that when you have decided upon an outcome, there is but that outcome; that which you have decided upon. Anything else is not a decision.

Evidently, deciding comes with a sense of certainty. How, then, do you create that sense of certainty? When you decide, you are literally, deliberately, and purposely changing your state of consciousness, which is the same as changing who you are. Therefore, a state of consciousness and a state of being, are interchangeable terms. Deciding on purpose is changing from who you are now to who you want to be. For example, a change of state is required to go from medical student to medical doctor; a process that may have begun with a childhood ambition and a decision.

Sadly, many of our decisions are not personal conclusions but adopted opinions, which have us living lives imposed on us by the will of others—like my cardiologist friend in London, who I mentioned in a previous chapter.

It's Never Too Late to Decide

The most liberating thing about education is not the certificate at the end of it, even if it does help you land the career of your dreams. No, the most liberating thing is the understanding and application of that education. One such example for me was learning about the *theory of second best* as an economics undergraduate, back in the day. The theory holds that there are situations in which optimal conditions are not available, so the next-best conditions that are available become the new optimal.

> *"The best time to plant a tree is twenty years ago. The second-best time is now."*
>
> —**Ancient proverb**

In economics, the theory may apply well to a region of the country where the skilled labor force required for a particular business operation simply does not exist. So, the best of what does exist becomes the new optimal.

Applying the theory of second best to the attainment of your worthy ideal, we might say that the optimal conditions for you were twenty years ago, when you were single and had no children; when your health was better; when you had so much less invested in your current career; or, when your financial resources were more plentiful. If, today, the optimal conditions you imagine no longer exist, they are no longer optimal. Your present circumstances, whatever they may be, are the new optimal. What was liberating for me in this lesson was that I didn't have to stop at second best, third best, or next best. Liberation was knowing that every moment provides optimal conditions. The past and future do not exist. Too many people allow these apparently optimal parallel existences—the past and the future—to rob themselves of their opportunity to improve their lives, because doing so can only ever be done *now*.

Imagine That

Physics has long since demonstrated conclusively that everything in the universe, from a chicken to a brick, is fundamentally energy. The countless differences observed come from the different vibrational rates (energy frequencies) of these objects. Furthermore, the frequency of energy within varieties of the same type also differs: our medical student and our medical doctor; a successful salesperson and her unsuccessful coworker; the dedicated parent and their indifferent counterpart.

The main quality that makes one person successful and another unsuccessful is not any of the usual suspects most observers turn to: willpower, natural ability, heredity, environment, role models, etc. It is *imagination*. And, more importantly, *creative* imagination. Like you, a grasshopper can "image"—that is, create a picture of—its outer circumstances. This is seeing with the eye. Unlike you, however, it cannot imagine, which is seeing *through* the eye. *Imaging* is responding to what is about you; *imagining* is creating what you want about you. Our grasshopper's decisions are all responsive, whereas your *best* decisions are creative.

Creative imagination is not simply the ability to form a mental picture, so to speak. It is the creation of a future, an outcome, of circumstances you *choose*. It is this ability to imagine that affects the rate at which you vibrate and, therefore, the consciousness you adopt. Everyone imagines, but it is the skillful use of imagination that creates the outcomes you desire. This skillful use of imagination requires focused attention, which is a critical component in the neuro·ADAPT·ive Programming creation process, which I will discuss in-depth later in the book.

Small is the Gate and Narrow the Road

If you're wondering why so few decide to do what they really want, let me tell you why: we do not live in a vacuum. There are many influences affecting us this way and that. They are the very ones mentioned earlier, such as not having enough time or money, or not being good-looking enough. What you have to do is forget about all the reasons why you can't achieve the outcome you really

> *Imaging is responding to what is about you; imagining is creating what you want about you.*

want. You create what you pay attention to, even if it is what you don't want. If I tell you, "Don't think of a red bus," I can be certain that you will think of a red bus. Overindulgence in negative news items concerning violence, illness, scarcity, or other negative situations will ensure that your attention is directed to where you may not want it to be. If your attention is focused on what you don't want, it won't be focused on what you *do* want. Pay attention to the sage advice of not being able to simultaneously serve two masters.

Be aware that you aren't alone in not having all the answers upfront. Einstein didn't have all the answers for his theories of relativity before he proved them. Edison didn't know how to create an electric light bulb. It didn't stop them from pursuing their ambitions—and thank God! Edison had to fail over ten thousand times before he finally got it! Not one of the ordinary people like you and me, whom I've coached over the years and who had extraordinary ambitions, knew how to achieve them until they began their pursuit. The amazing thing that always seems to happen is that as you move toward your goal, more of it is revealed to you, like the detail of a mountain coming into view, the closer you get to it.

Rather than focus on all the reasons you can't achieve your worthy ideal, make a list of all the reasons you *can* start toward it, and can achieve it, no matter how small or how unlikely any given reason may seem. Something that is seemingly insignificant now, may take on much greater significance while you're along the way. Add as many new ideas to the list as they come to you. Review this list regularly—at least daily. Focused attention is a critical component of creation.

Your Fulfilling Life Action Assignment

1. A lack of commitment is often why a goal is delayed or left unfulfilled. Think of something you've repeatedly failed to achieve. How committed are you to achieving it? Is it a worthy ideal, or something you feel obliged to do because of others' opinions, or your own unclear thinking about it?

2. Create your worthy ideal statement and start using it immediately.

3. Make a list of at least five reasons you *will* achieve your worthy ideal.

CHAPTER SIX

Your Quantum Leap

Responsibility and Reciprocity

With the freedom to decide comes great responsibility. You are free to create both good and bad; however, what you put out is what you shall receive in kind, according to the law of karma. This is a hugely significant point. At the lower end of intelligent life, there is little deviation from what is considered to be average in the advancement within a species. Yet, look at the deviation within humanity: at one end, you have individuals imagining, designing, and erecting soaring towers; harnessing the power inherent within the atom; uncovering the secrets of electromagnetism; turning sand into microprocessors to enable near-instantaneous worldwide communication; devising mathematical equations that reveal nature's nudity; and so on. Meanwhile, at the other end of the spectrum of humanity, you have individuals who, although of sound mind, are wasting away on the couch instead of attempting to create the life they truly want. This contrasts with the difference in the capacities of, say, salmon, for which you may measure individuals' varying strengths to swim upstream, or their prowess for reproduction.

The more advanced a species, the greater its burden of responsibility to execute item number one on the agenda of spirit's mission statement: create good in the world. The same is true of the most advanced within a species. In a sense, this can be likened to a corporation in which the CEO, when compared to the office clerk, has a greater responsibility to the stockholders to deliver on the corporation's mission statement.

Homo sapiens is Latin for "wise man," which is more commonly articulated as "thinking person" in contemporary vocabulary. This "thinking" designation distinguishes modern humans as highly innovative, advanced thinkers, distinct from their several less advanced thinking predecessors like *homo erectus* and *homo neanderthalensis*. An examination of modern history provides reasonable testimony that the most advanced thinkers have been the most prolific contributors to the betterment of humanity: Helen Keller, Mahatma Gandhi, Mary Baker Eddy, Shakespeare, Marie Curie, Steve Jobs, Sir Isaac Newton, Socrates, Jane Austen, Galileo, Mother Teresa, Mozart, Florence Nightingale...The important point here is not to pay homage to, but to learn from these luminaries so that you too may improve the quality (measured in goodness), and the quantity (measured by service to others) of your own contributions. Improving these contributions requires great responsibility on your part.

The word *responsibility* implies that there are no excuses (only reasons) for the circumstances of your life, and that there is no one else to blame for those circumstances. When you adopt this attitude toward responsibility, you no longer regard spiritual growth as a means to achieving your worthy ideal. Instead, you realize that spiritual growth is, in itself, your highest purpose through which the truest meaning for your life is revealed.

Through spiritual growth, you become the person who can accomplish your worthy ideal, thereby living a more fulfilling life.

The Most Influential Aspect of Spiritual Growth

There is one common denominator among persons who lead extremely fulfilling lives and contribute greatly to humanity: love. Typically, when you think of the word *love*, you get the impression that it is something felt about someone or something, and that is fine. However, you can go deeper to find a much richer vein. In chapter 4, we discussed how love, to the enlightened, is a state of consciousness. You feel love for and give love to a person or thing to the extent to which you *are* love itself. You can feel and give no more than you are. This brings us back to karma and the law of attraction.

Now, let us apply this idea of being love to your worthy ideal. If the worthy ideal is something you feel just okay about, your tendency will be to put out okay energy and receive, in return, okay results (karma). You will also attract an okay amount of energy in the form of the people, resources, and opportunities you come across in the process of pursuing your worthy ideal. It is no wonder, then, that the successful have time and again counseled us to engage in activities, careers, and vocations that we love, should we truly aspire to the success we claim to desire. To achieve a lot, you must love a lot.

When the enlightened heart becomes love, it is elevated to express its lovingness even in the darkest of times. While our hearts may never reach such elevated heights, it pays to express the greatest love that we can for our worthy ideal. Understanding that you are as likely to face

> *It is no wonder, then, that the successful have time and again counseled us to engage in activities, careers, and vocations that we love, should we truly aspire to the success we claim to desire.*

ridicule as you are recognition, will help you to keep your sanity. When things get tough, as they sometimes will, the extent of your inoculation against the naysayers will be equal to your love for your worthy ideal.

Right-Thinking

Much of the difference between humanity's great achievers and the rest is the applied knowledge of how to think correctly, particularly when it comes to creative imagination. The brightest minds throughout history have counseled us on the importance of right-thinking:

> *"Your time is limited, so don't waste it living someone else's life. Don't be trapped by dogma—which is living with the results of other people's thinking. Don't let the noise of others' opinions drown out your own inner voice. And most important, have the courage to follow your heart and intuition."*
>
> —**Steve Jobs**

Intellect is a faculty of the conscious mind. It can be measured in several ways, two of which are Intelligence Quotient (IQ) and Emotional Intelligence (EQ) testing. Unlike intellect (mental intelligence), we don't know how to measure inspiration (spiritual intelligence)—a faculty of the subconscious mind. The meaning of the word *inspiration* in the context used here is "divine influence." The most profound thinking requires both intellect and inspiration. Inspiration is most available to us during meditation and contemplation, when the body is still (or rhythmic, like when running or walking) and the mind is quiet. We may refer to this state as *no-thinking*.

Creating a fulfilling life is best achieved when applying the inspiration from no-thinking to the intellect of right-thinking. The inspirational ideas, visions, and thoughts gained from the subconscious during meditation, for example, are glimpses of the truth within you. We saw in chapter 4, in the section titled *From External Reality to Internal Truth*, that we should allow internal truth to guide external reality. A lot more will be said about this in chapter 10, which examines the laws of creation. These inspirational, subconscious truths can be consciously channeled by the intellect toward achieving your fulfilling life on purpose, through the application of neuro·ADAPT·ive Programming. Doing so provides the quantum leap we are looking for.

A Wormhole to Every Dream

To clarify the point, let me share a metaphor. Imagine a fully crewed spacecraft, lost in space and trekking its way home as best it can. Let's suppose that with its present capabilities (level of intellect), its journey home will take many light-years. By improving propulsion capacity—which we may liken to IQ—a light-year or so may be wiped off the journey; by developing better astronomical charts—which we may liken to EQ—a bit more may be wiped off; and by cross-training the crew, the time can be reduced even further; and so on. However, the dim prospect is that the journey remains one of many light-years. On returning home, the crew that pilots the ship into the earth's atmosphere will be the distant offspring of the one that began the journey. What is required, instead, is a quantum leap; something beyond the conventional, that ignores the existence of spacetime. What is required is a wormhole—a shortcut home. A similar quantum leap is available to create your fulfilling life on purpose, and that is the neuro·ADAPT·ive Programming process.

As a faculty of the conscious mind, intellect is used to

put information into your conscious mind. You study the information from without. It is the capacity to learn and to reason, and is therefore operated in activity, in *doing*. It is a faculty of corporeal existence, which is both temporal and finite.

Inspiration is a faculty of the subconscious mind. Unlike intellect, you do not *use* inspiration; it is experienced from within and drawn out of you. Inspiration is inherent in the unconscious depths of the eternal, omniscient subconscious. It operates in inactivity, in *being*. Through inspiration, you know a thing because it exists. It is a part of spirit; and, as such, you have access to it via your subconscious—subjective conscious—mind.

Subconscious knowledge is *revealed*—is revelation—by inspiration. Inspiration is what unreasonable persons who persist in trying to adapt the world to themselves cherish above all else, for it is what allows them to shape the world. Submitting your worthy ideal to the subconscious mind with the neuro·ADAPT·ive Programming process is like accessing the wormhole, and the wormhole is inspiration. The subconscious has solutions you cannot discover with intellect; It is the stuff of dreams, and the dream maker, all at once. Because the subconscious is eternal, it works *with* the eternal. In doing so, it can obtain a solution from anywhere in eternity—any place in the past, present, or the future—to solve a present-day problem. And while this might sound too fantastic to be true, there it is. Individuals under hypnosis have described, in colorful detail, past events that they could have no conscious knowledge of. Even more profound, though, is their ability to disclose future events that they could have no conscious knowledge of. The fact that not everyone under hypnosis is touched by divine influence is beside the point. The point is that divine influence is available, and if available to John Smith, it's also available to Mary Jones. Divinity does not play favorites.

Your Fulfilling Life Action Assignment

1. a. What unwanted experiences tend to recur in your life?

   b. Why do you think they recur and what can you do to prevent them from doing so?

   For example, a client of mine complained about not being listened to by others. When analyzed, we found the reasons were that he complained excessively, was extremely opinionated, and was judgmental of others. To remedy the situation, I asked him to journal each episode of feeling unheard that he experienced. By doing so, he was able to determine whether it was specific individuals that he complained at, had strong opinions about, and was judgmental of. Some did feel the brunt of his negativity more than others, but only because he had to interact with them more than others. His negative behaviors were definitely general character traits. This knowledge, and the will to change, allowed him to take a pause before interacting with others, so that he could mentally step back and be more considered in what he said, and how he said it, especially during important meetings. With further journaling, he was able to track an improvement in his being listened to, as a direct result of his new behaviors.

   c. How can you change your thinking to eradicate these unwanted experiences?

2. a. How much in love are you with the worthy ideal you decided on from chapter 4?

b. Does thinking about this worthy ideal get you excited—perhaps even a mixture of excitement and fear?

c. If you don't get excited and are perhaps a little fearful, reexamine whether you have the right worthy ideal.

3. Create a short statement about thinking that motivates you to elevate your thinking. An example of this would be what another client created for himself to good effect: *"Every positive conscious thought I submit to my subconscious mind improves my life in ways I could not otherwise imagine."*

CHAPTER SEVEN

The Nature of Spirit

Defining the Indefinable

In this chapter I'm attempting the impossible, and that is to define something indefinable—the infinite and eternal, an obviously self-defeating endeavor. That something is "spirit".

> "The Tao that can be told is not the eternal Tao;
> The name that can be named is not the eternal name."
> —Lao Tzu

Being that spirit is infinite and eternal, the best I can do in defining it is to say that spirit *is*, and that, really, is where I ought to leave well enough alone. Spirit *is*. The addition of descriptive words limits the limitless. This leads to the conclusion that spirit cannot be known by the mind or through physical senses. The body-mind realms adhere to the principle that seeing is believing, whereas the spiritual understanding is that *believing* leads to *seeing*. There is a very important distinction here. In the former case, we are expecting effects to reveal causes; in the latter, we acknowledge that internal causes produce and, therefore, precede external effects.

> "A significant reason for life's challenges is that we are continually tinkering with effects in the hope of producing better ones, rather than creating new causes that will produce the effects that we want."

A significant reason for life's challenges is that we are continually tinkering with effects in the hope of producing better ones, rather than creating new causes that will produce the effects that we want. An example would be changing a diet to lose weight. Intellectually, this seems to be a logical course of action. Depending on which study you believe, somewhere between 80 and 92 percent of all New Year's resolutions are broken. Given how many of those resolutions are about losing weight, it is reasonable to assume that the failure rate for dieting is similar.

Indeed, a *Psychology Today* study showed that the failure rate of dieters is 95 percent. A National Institutes of Health study of fourteen contestants participating in the *Biggest Loser* reality TV show concluded that all but one regained weight within the six-year study period, even though they continued their regimens of diet and exercise. That's a 93 percent failure rate. Many other studies across different nations have produced similar results to the two cited here.

These results could be significantly improved by incorporating spirit into the process. The late Maxwell Maltz, a cosmetic surgeon, and creator of Psycho-Cybernetics (a system to improve self-image), found time and again that if a patient's self-image was unhealthy or faulty, all their efforts would end in failure. They'd feel the same way about themselves as they did prior to cosmetic surgery. This explains why, even though the National Institutes of Health study's participants changed behavior, their results were ultimately unchanged.

So, the key to improving results is changing how you think about yourself in relation to those results. In this instance, you must ignore the physical reality of being overweight and instead embrace the spiritual truth of being your desired weight and shape. Even so, lasting shifts in thinking are not achieved by just trying to think differently, i.e., thinking of yourself as slim instead of overweight. If it were that easy, diets would be way more successful. The causal relationship is as follows:

Spiritual disciplines effect new ways of thinking, and these new ways of thinking in turn create new behaviors that become habitual, thereby producing improved, lasting results.

You will learn more about how to create these lasting changes in the final two chapters, which are dedicated to neuro·ADAPT·ive Programming, our principal tool for purposely creating a fulfilling life.

For now, it's important to know that the spiritual realm—the place of primal causes—is experienced only when stilling the body and quieting the mind. Meditation, then, is the ultimate medium by which we may experience the spiritual realm. In meditation we can receive spiritual guidance to improve our lives. With neuro·ADAPT·ive Programming, we direct the subconscious mind to improve our lives.

In defining the indefinable, I want to consider just three of many attributes of spirit: principle, unity, and love.

Spirit as Principle

In the spiritual realm, principles are infinite and eternal. Two of the best proofs of this come from numbers and shapes. It doesn't matter in what quadrant of the universe you live, or when in the past, present, or future you live, one plus one will always equal two. The concept of a circle is unchanging and without beginning or end. As concepts, numbers and shapes are perfect. In other words, you cannot improve on one plus one equaling two. You cannot improve a circle by introducing another property to it—

perhaps a straight line or a kink. To do so creates something other than a circle.

These concepts cannot be attributed to the realms of either body or mind since, being infinite and eternal, they exist in spite of, and prior to, the existence of both. They are exclusively spiritual concepts. There is nothing you can do to corrupt their spiritual perfection; they just *are*. However, when we apply these perfect concepts to the realms of body and mind, corruption becomes possible and often likely. We are very capable of incorrect mental mathematics, writing a number down incorrectly, and drawing imperfect circles.

From these examples, we may infer that the spiritual realm is one of perfection, and that it is only when we apply spiritual concepts in the realms of body and mind that they can become corruptible. The goal, then, is to raise your conscious awareness so that your conscious and subconscious minds harmoniously interpret the spiritual concepts (worthy ideal) you want to manifest, like achieving your ideal weight. The results of doing so will be reflected in your actions, improving the circumstances of your life. When your thinking and actions conform with your worthy ideal, you are purposely creating your fulfilling life.

Getting on track requires the relinquishing of all concerns about outer appearances. When your current circumstances are a mismatch with those you desire, remember that what you *do* want already exists, perfectly, within your spiritual realm. Making decisions on what you want, rather than on what you have, will enable you to realize your spiritual perfection in your mental and physical realms. So, don't judge the tree by the bark that it wears, but by the fruit that it bears. There are seasons when that fruit is invisible on the tree...but you know it is coming. Sometimes that fruit is bitter, like in a failure. In such cases it is well to remember the sage advice of the herbalists of old: the more bitter the medicine, the greater its power to heal; so, you carry on toward your worthy ideal in the full expectation of it coming to pass.

When we truly understand that principle is an attribute of spirit, miracles are no longer things which are inexplicable by natural laws and explicable only by considering divine intervention. Instead, they are considered to be the workings of spiritual principles that materialize in the body-mind realms in ways that we do not understand. Many modern marvels were considered miraculous before we understood the principles behind the so-called miracles. To name a few, we have:

- Helium balloons appearing to defy the principle of gravity, but actually confirming it;
- Aluminum structures riding on airwaves;
- Lumps of steel floating on water;
- Electrically powered bulbs illuminating the world;
- Wireless communication; and
- stem cell therapy.

You will need courage to create your fulfilling life. You will likely have to confront your fears and a portion of the world, the size of which will depend on the size of your worthy ideal. You must ignore what others think about who you are and what you want. Often, you must also relinquish many social rules and customs that do not serve the attainment of your fulfilling life.

> *Remember, Galileo was considered crazy for saying things his society thought were abominations against religion. Take their jest with a grain of salt and stride with confidence. Don't fall into the trap society has laid out for anyone willing to challenge the norm.*
> —**Robin Sharma**

Spirit as Unity

To explore and explain spiritual unity, I'm going to use some ideas from quantum mechanics (without getting too scientific).

Symmetry is the term quantum mechanics uses to describe the interconnectedness of the forces and fields of nature. Wherever you see the word *symmetry*, think *unity*. Symmetry maintains that just prior to the Big Bang and the resulting creation of the universe, all of the forces and fields of nature were unified as one beautiful whole. Today, those fields and forces are separate—electric, magnetic, strong nuclear, weak nuclear, and gravitation. This separateness is called *asymmetry,* or broken symmetry. It is a discrimination of parts within the whole.

A preoccupation of contemporary physicists is the unification (reunification, really) of the forces and fields of nature into one model, which they refer to as the Theory of Everything (TOE). Physicists believe the TOE model would confirm the interconnectedness of everything in the universe and explain its entire workings in one mathematical formula.

The human similarity with the notion of symmetry is that our bodies and minds represent broken symmetry like the individual fields and forces of nature, but underlying this broken symmetry is spirit, which preserves symmetry and unity. In the spiritual realm, we are one interconnected whole; the phenomenon that connects us all is universal consciousness.

Psychologists and philosophers regard universal consciousness (or mind) as the underlying essence of all existence and creation in the universe, including that which occurred prior to the creation and existence of humanity as physical and mental beings. The body-mind

> *Knowing this, we might ask, "Is the ice in the water, or the water in the ice?"*

realms are said to be the manifestations of universal consciousness, and so, *man*-ifestation is created in the image and likeness of God (consciousness). In other words, spirit is the cause of our lives' circumstances, including our bodies and minds. The difference between what we consider to be a person's individual consciousness and universal consciousness is akin to the comparison between a droplet of water and the ocean.

Two things we know philosophically about infinity are that it is indivisible, and it cannot be multiplied. To divide infinity by, say, the number two, would (theoretically) yield two infinities, or two halves of infinity. Of course, both these terms are nonsensical. If, conversely, we multiply infinity by the number two, we get an infinity twice as large, which again is nonsensical, as to do so would be to acknowledge that the first infinity could not have been infinite. Therefore, by extension, the second infinity wouldn't be infinite either, because it would have been proven to be divisible by two.

Spirit is infinite. Its manifestation into multifarious forms should not, therefore, be seen, as its own self-division into individual units. What we perceive as individual things, be they animal, mineral or vegetable, are simply expressions of the unseen spiritual whole. Because unity is a spiritual characteristic, it can be difficult to grasp intellectually. This unity is best experienced in meditation. My own intellectual understanding of this concept is improved when I imagine spirit to be the Arctic Ocean, complete with distinguishable pieces of ice. Knowing this, we might ask, "Is the ice in the water, or the water in the ice?" The answer to both questions is, of course, "yes." We may take the metaphor further by saying that the ice is an expression of the water, just as the body and mind, and everything else in the physical universe, are expressions of spirit. What we observe as separateness is what Einstein referred to as "a kind of optical delusion of consciousness." Our five senses and mind are not perceptive enough to notice and therefore experience the oneness of all creation. Even so, we are, in the truest sense, eternally one with everything: past, present, and future.

> "A human being is a part of the whole, called by us "Universe," a part limited in time and space. He experiences himself, his thoughts and feelings as something separated from the rest—a kind of optical delusion of his consciousness. The striving to free oneself from this delusion is the one issue of true religion. Not to nourish the delusion but to try to overcome it is the way to reach the attainable measure of peace of mind."
>
> —**Einstein**

It is difficult to rationalize, but your individual consciousness and the collective consciousness of humanity have far-reaching consequences in both time and space, and in the most mind-boggling sense, affecting all of creation that ever was, is, and shall be. So, it is reasonable to infer that all things are immersed in some medium or substance that enables your consciousness to cohere with mine, and for humanity's collective consciousness to impact the physical world in general.

An example of the effects of individual consciousness is provided in a paper titled *Feeling the Future: Experimental Evidence for Anomalous Retroactive Influences on Cognition and Affect*, by Daryl Bem, social psychologist and professor emeritus at Cornell University. It provides statistical evidence that telepathy, clairvoyance, and psychokinesis are real phenomena that should be taken seriously.

> *"When you have eliminated the impossible, whatever remains, however improbable, must be the truth."*
>
> —Arthur Conan Doyle, **Sherlock Holmes**

Bem's experiments are not the first to be scientifically based in this arena. The British and American Societies for Psychical Research, both established in the late 1800s, have amassed a lot of research data evidencing the existence of such phenomena, generally known as *psi* (pronounced *sigh*). However, the publication of Bem's research in the prestigious *Journal of Personality and Social Psychology*, together with generous column inches in *Psychology Today*, have piqued the interest of the pragmatic scientific community, encouraging it to take this area of study more seriously.

What of the effects of our collective consciousness? The Global Consciousness Project (GCP) is a parapsychology study which started at Princeton University in 1998. The project was set up to determine what effects, if any, global consciousness has on the physical world. In other words, does the collective mind of humanity create observable effects in the world?

Since its inception at Princeton, the project has become a study of international, multidisciplinary collaboration of around one hundred scientists and engineers. The GCP's maxim reads:

> *"Coherent consciousness creates order in the world. Subtle interactions link us with each other and the earth."*

The basic idea is that when human consciousness becomes coherent from major global events that engage our collective hearts and minds, the behavior of random systems such as weather patterns, the global economy, and social structures will change.

The sophisticated techniques used by the GCP normally produce completely unpredictable sequences of zeroes and ones. However, when a significant event, for example, the 9/11 terrorist attacks or a devastating tsunami, occurs, these unpredictable sequences become subtly structured. GCP officials calculate the odds of such structured events occurring by chance to be one in a trillion. Instead, they say, "The evidence suggests an emerging noosphere [sphere of human consciousness] or the unifying field of consciousness described by sages in all cultures."

The work of Bem and that of the GCP indicate the direct effects that individual and collective consciousness, respectively, have on our world. The GCP apart, one failing of most psi research is that it attributes the phenomena to the body-mind realms by concluding that they must be attributable to some form of biochemical brain function. The scientific community's conviction that seeing is believing prevents it from considering the invisible spiritual realm for the results it observes and publishes for psi phenomena. If you're looking for your eyeglasses in the wrong room, you'll never find them. As I previously stated, believing precedes seeing in the spiritual realm. Therefore, psi results, as with accurately predicting the value of hidden playing cards or what someone else is thinking, are improved when the subject believes it's possible to predict those results. The results are predictable because of the unity of spirit, and not because of some unknown biochemical brain function. The wise counsel that emerges from these results is that you should be certain of taking responsibility for how you apply yourself—mind, body, and spirit—in creating your fulfilling life.

By no means is this discussion about psi an argument for or against the use of the High Street psychic. That rests with your good judgment. Suffice it to say, after using a psychic many years ago, all I could think of while handing over a pile of my hard-earned cash was, "She must have seen me coming!" No, this discussion is, rather, an argument that psi phenomena (and I will include spiritual healing here) do not work by magic or miracle. Like balloons appearing to defy the principle of gravity and lumps of steel floating on water, they work by infallible principles. As yet, we do not fully understand these principles, but as with those that govern the use of electricity, we know enough to use them to improve the circumstances of our lives. They work because of the spiritual unity of all things. In other words, we do not each have a spirit; we all share *the* communal spirit, which some call God, some call Allah, others call universal consciousness, and so on.

Intentionally tapping into universal consciousness enables us to attract things that are consistent with our own level of consciousness, by the law of attraction. This is the purpose of neuro-ADAPT-ive Programming; its potency comes from applying what we do understand about spiritual principles to purposely create a fulfilling life.

Physicist John Steward Bell established the principle of nonlocality as a general feature of the universe. Sometimes called action at a distance, nonlocality claims that particle A can somehow communicate instantaneously with particle B, regardless of distance. This means that the speed of communication between A and B ignores the universal speed limit, or light speed.

The authenticity of nonlocality has been verified. In experiments, the measurement of one photon has simultaneously changed the nature (known as polarization) of another photon, with no regard for space or time. The photons' behavior is suggestive of an eternal existence beyond the effects of space and time. Something links the pair in such a way that, as one physicist remarked, when one is tickled, the other one laughs. Like psi phenomena, nonlocal influences do not diminish with distance.

If we regard the two photons as individual entities separated in space and time, contrary to Einstein's theory of relativity, information is passing from one photon to the other at unlimited speed. Also, time for these photons is independent of their relative positions or velocities. However, Einstein's equations predict otherwise. In this scenario, the photons' time is eternal. Alternatively, they are inseparably connected by something invisible, a feature of which is perfect, instantaneous communication.

Is humanity's existence the subject of such unity through the medium of universal consciousness?

The late physicist John Wheeler put forward an idea that one electron formed the entire universe. His assumptions were based on the findings of one of quantum mechanics' most prolific theories, quantum electrodynamics (QED), which describes how light and matter interact. It is the first quantum theory to be fully consistent with Einstein's special relativity theory. When I first read about this, I was so astonished that I couldn't shake the idea from my mind. During a period of meditation, it caused me to imagine that I was riding at the head of a light beam, having a conversation with a photon. This is how it went:

Conversation With a Photon

Asleep one night I had a dream,
I saw a light, a shooting beam.
On and on the light beam shone,
until I met with a photon,
Existing here inside the beam,
One of billions, or so it seemed.

For then it was that time stood still,
And space, in distance, equaled nil.

It asked of me, "What is your crime?
You seem to still be in your prime.
So why are you here doing time?"

I asked of it, "Where are you from?"
"Here and there and everywhere,
Existing since the dawn of time;
A punishment for all my crime."

"And what crime, pray, did you commit?"
"I dared to dream that I exist,
For which my Maya does persist."

"Don't understand. What do you mean?"
"It's no difficult conclusion.
All about you is illusion."

"I'm still adrift in some confusion,
About what you call this illusion."

"What you see as you and me,
Is really just one unity.

We are the same old speck of dust,
Doing as we think we must.
As QED will attest,
I create at God's behest.
All the beauty that you see,
Has emanated just from me."

Then it asked: "What is the time?"
"I think it's 1999."
"Are you sure?
Where has it gone?
There's a big bang where I come from."

"If it is as you say,
Why some sad while others gay?
Why some rich and others poor?
Why are some above the law?"

"I don't know, but then I'd guess,
You create the illusion that suits you best."

Then I woke upon my bed,
Recalling what the photon said,
Thinking of the life I've led,
Oh, what could I have done instead?

Spirit as Love

The three attributes of spirit are inextricably bound, such that they really are one phenomenon, each being incapable of existence apart from the others. The spiritual principle is love and it is a principle because, spiritually, we are one. So, this triad may be regarded as the One Truth—spiritual perfection—from which we each create our personal reality. The proximity of your personal reality to the One Truth is dependent on what you place your faith in.

The effects of loving (or not loving) your neighbor as yourself are inevitable and beyond human intervention due to karma. So, what we call a commandment is, in fact, an unfailing law. The law is that you can love your neighbor only as much as you love yourself, and yet, I believe that the matter is more complex than first appearances suggest. From personal introspection and from my experience coaching others, I've come to realize that you cannot love another more than you love yourself in specific areas of your life. Let me explain.

When we love who we are in a relationship context, we tend to truly want the best for other people in their relationships, to the same extent we love ourselves. When we dislike who we are in relationships, we may outwardly express goodwill toward others in relationships but, when we check our internal compass, we may find that our goodwill is expressed through the proverbial gritted teeth. The reason for this is that subconscious insecurities, fears, and so on are stored as a complex around the general context of relationships. This complex controls your feelings, decisions and behaviors.

Loving who we are in a business context through success in that arena, we find ourselves genuinely expressing goodwill toward others in business (I'm ignoring the psychological effects on some businesspersons caused by what they may perceive as a direct competitor).

It will be no surprise for you to hear me say that many successful businesspeople simultaneously experience poor relationships, while many who enjoy successful relationships are serial business failures. It is possible, then, to simultaneously want the best for others in

> **When operating from the body-mind realms alone, we tend to like those we perceive to be similar to ourselves, both culturally and in other ways.**

business while not feeling the same way about others in relationships, and vice versa. The controlling complexes generate these contrary loving attitudes, sabotaging our conscious desires. The subconscious is the ultimate lie detector; it discovers our unconscious self-deceptions with extraordinary precision.

There are three other barriers preventing us from loving others as we are called to by various religious traditions. The first is misunderstanding love to be an emotion that binds us to the object of our love. No human can simultaneously hate someone and be bound to them with the so-called emotion of love. The spiritual expression of love is wanting the best for everyone. Wanting the best for someone is wanting them to achieve their highest level of consciousness. Such spiritual growth is the answer to all of the world's evils, the underlying principle of which is love.

The second additional barrier is not recognizing the unity of all. We look at our neighbor and our enemy and perceive only individual physical and personality characteristics, which we like or dislike. When operating from the body-mind realms alone, we tend to like those we perceive to be similar to ourselves, both culturally and in other ways. But, regardless of outer appearances, what we think of others affects them and, in return, reflects back on ourselves. Like our photons, when we are tickled, our neighbor laughs and we smile in return. Conversely, if we pinch, our neighbor is pained and so are we. The effects of outer appearances on your behavior can be lessened by remembering that the truth about your neighbor is spiritual, so cannot be seen; and also, remembering that what you do see is your personal interpretation of reality, of that spiritual truth. Spirit is without gender, race, color, creed, religion, political preference, national allegiance, wealth, or poverty. It just *is*.

> "We shall never get blacks and whites, or Orientals and Occidentals, to unite by trying to tie the different branches of the human tree together with string. Attention must instead be shifted to the stem and the root, where, under the surface, we are one."

—Alan Watts, **Cloud-Hidden Whereabouts Unknown**

Realizing the spiritual nature of all, you will see the good in all. You will separate the act from the actor and know that however bad the act, that the actor is essentially good.

The third additional barrier is a belief that loving our enemy, especially, is a religious practice, even when we may not want anything to do with religion. But to love your neighbor and your enemy as suggested is not a principle that belongs to any religion. It is a spiritual truth, divinely revealed and wisely adopted by various religious traditions.

Even the most fleeting glance at world affairs will confirm that, of ourselves, we cannot love our enemies and pray for those who would persecute us. We have to rely on the Creator's (spirit's) love, which enables us to be loving. So, it is to spirit that we must turn in meditation to gain the resources to be loving. First, we get that love for ourselves because of the nature of the principle: we can love others only to the extent that we love ourselves. Our increasing self-love can then be increasingly expressed toward others, and as we do unto those others, similar things are done unto us by the law of karma.

The greatest expression of love is forgiveness. It releases a balm that elevates the forgiver's spiritual awareness, narrowing the gap between their personal reality and the One Truth. As such, forgiveness is, counterintuitively, more beneficial to the forgiver than it is to the one being forgiven. This is especially the case when it comes to the forgiveness of our enemies.

> *Virtue pardons the wicked, as the sandal tree perfumes the axe which strikes it.*
>
> **—Medieval Persian poet, Saadi of Shiraz**

Regardless of what we have done, spirit allows us to start over anew by the agency of repentance. To repent is not to beg the Creator for forgiveness, but to turn from sin toward righteousness, where righteousness is thinking correctly of the spiritual principles from which right actions flow, and sin is thinking and the consequent actions that lead away from what is righteous.

Repentance and forgiveness are two sides of the same coin. Forgiveness is the certain consequence of repentance, just as getting wet is the certain consequence of being in water.

"Forgive us our sins as we forgive others" is not a commandment but a law. The law is that we can forgive others only to the extent that we forgive ourselves, just as we can only love others as we love ourselves.

Self-love can be problematic because of past hurts that have created an unhealthy or faulty self-image.

Let's look at a real-life, practical example from earlier in the book: the difficulty of achieving permanent weight loss. We've already seen that empirical studies dismiss the idea that losing weight is always simply a matter of moving more and eating less. So, we can now consider some of the more deep-seated reasons for being unable to permanently shed the pounds. The reasons are varied and psychologically based; they include depression, stress, boredom, anxiety, frustration, and shame. These are particularly potent when resulting from a psychological trauma like sexual abuse, school bullying, parental neglect, spousal rejection, and familial death.

Any of these traumatic events can cause a psychological hunger for attention that manifests in the bodily realm as a hunger for food, resulting in excessive weight gain.

Many years ago, I had an exceptionally beautiful coaching client who had gained weight because she didn't want to attract attention, due to psychological trauma from childhood sexual abuse. It was by divine grace rather than any skill on my part that, together, we discovered this causal relationship; she wasn't able to overcome the shame that came from the abuse. Openly she craved intimacy; subconsciously she despised the idea. As with all things, the subconscious feelings ruled. Chapter 9 on the effects of faith and fear provides a detailed discussion on why this is so.

Our work in overcoming her subconscious complex included the following strategies:

- The creation of a mantra that best expressed what she really wanted;
- A visualization of what her life would look like when she got it;
- Combining the mantra and visualization as a prayer;
- Taking this prayer into contemplative meditation;
- And lastly, going into silent meditation where this prayer would work on a spiritual level.

We did not discuss dieting. Her excessive weight was a symptom (an effect) of her complex. The cause was subconscious and had to be addressed within the spiritual realm for self-forgiveness to occur.

Within nine months, she went from weighing around 180 pounds to 135 pounds, with no discernible change in diet or exercise regimen.

Let me stress that I'm a huge advocate of healthy eating and a sensible exercise regimen, based on the counsel of experts in these fields. Yet, without a spiritual base, diet and exercise can be limited in their effectiveness.

Another client, on marrying "Mrs. Right," immediately started to gain weight. Again, there were no discernible changes in diet or exercise regimens for the weight gain— or the eventual weight loss that occurred.

This man was extremely handsome with a magnetic personality, a combination that made him very attractive to women. Prior to marrying, he had been involved in many romantic relationships. A recurring theme in our coaching sessions was an underlying sense of dread that he felt. There was no apparent reason for this. I asked him to pose the simple question, "Why am I afraid?" before each daily five-minute meditation practice, and imagine that the question was being submitted to his subconscious, which would give him a definite answer in due course.

On his way to work one morning, he saw a billboard advertising toothpaste. It featured the smiling face of a woman. He immediately realized that his fear was of being unfaithful to his wife, given all the unsolicited attention he was accustomed to attracting from women. The subconscious anxiety to resist other women had manifested in the body realm as a barrier of fat cells.

I encouraged him to share this epiphany with his wife, believing that it—being off his chest and into the open light—would be released from his psyche, and so it proved. His wife did not take what he had shared as a threat but was comforted by his concern to remain faithful to her. He subsequently shed the excess weight as quickly as he had gained it.

In another case, this time of a family friend rather than a client, a woman started gaining weight without any discernible change in diet or exercise regimen, on becoming a grandparent for the first time. The weight gain and grandparenthood weren't automatically linked, but eventually, we managed to relate it to another childhood experience. Her own grandmother was, in her own words, plump. This person really liked how it felt when she hugged her grandmother. Subconsciously, she associated being plump with being a good grandmother; something she desperately wanted to be.

Is it possible to infer from these three examples that self-image can affect other areas of health and wellness— in particular, and more broadly, our relationships, finances, careers, and businesses? Absolutely. Your self-image sets up expectations that may become self-fulfilling prophecies.

Your Fulfilling Life Action Assignment

1. Maxwell Maltz found that if a patient's self-image was unhealthy or faulty, all that patient's efforts would end in failure. Consider:

   a. Whether your self-image supports or hinders your achieving your worthy ideal; and

   b. If the latter is the case, what qualities of self-image would help you to turn things around.

2. Einstein called our perception of being separate from everything else an "optical delusion" from which we must free ourselves. Develop an exercise to help free yourself of this delusion. One I use personally is to be

still and imagine I'm connected to everyone and everything; a bit like the Borg in *Star Trek*, but without the malice or desire to assimilate everyone. Once I'm in a state of oneness, I imagine and feel reciprocal love because of the good things I've done for others. I then feel sincere remorse for any harm I've done to others— I move quickly from remorse to feeling forgiven. In both cases, I imagine and feel my love spreading throughout the entire universe, blessing everyone and everything it touches. I believe that karmic law makes this more than just a futile mental exercise; it encourages me to think the best of others.

3. The first dieting example in this chapter gives some insight into the difficulty we might experience in forgiving ourselves, and how that unforgiveness can manifest in unwanted body-mind circumstances. Take some time to consider at least one unwanted circumstance in your life. What have you not forgiven yourself for? How might this be preventing you from changing? Now, forgive yourself. If appropriate, use solutions in the dieting examples given in this chapter to assist yourself in doing so.

CHAPTER EIGHT

The Most Important Question—Ever!

In the previous chapter, we considered spirit to be neutral—without gender, race, color, creed, religion, political preference, national allegiance, wealth, or poverty. This is a spirit that operates by unchanging principles, allowing the sun to shine on the just and the unjust, according to their respective faithfulness to those principles.

If we liken the Creator to a fire, we can say that the farther away you are from It (relationally), the less you will feel Its heat—love, grace, life, and unity. Getting too close to the fire is like believing you are a god unto yourself and you will get burned.

There are no favors with the Creator. Its heat warms the righteous, the sinner, the faithful, and the unfaithful in equal measure, according to their proximity to the fire (their faithfulness to spiritual principles). Needless to say, the righteous are closer to the fire than sinners, but there are no external obstacles preventing the sinner from getting closer to the fire. Forgiveness comes with repentance.

This impartial spirit may have previously been unfamiliar to you, so let's now consider spirit in more

> *life is seldom so straightforward as to afford a clear path on the way to wherever it is we think we're going.*

familiar terms and see what impact your ideas about spirit may be having on your life. As mentioned in the first chapter, I was raised Catholic. I'm still grateful for the disciplines that upbringing afforded, so this next piece is not a specific criticism of Catholicism; it is a personal confession of faith misplaced. No doubt, the sentiments it cites are just as applicable across innumerable faiths.

Being a diligent person, I believed in the saying, "God helps those who help themselves." This and similar beliefs allowed me to proactively take the initiative to improve my life. However, life is seldom so straightforward as to afford a clear path on the way to wherever it is we think we're going. I believed that the Creator wanted my unquestioning belief, but try as I might, I couldn't give it. How could I, when I also believed the Creator to be cruel for allowing little children to get diseases like leukemia, and die before they had the chance to live? I couldn't. So, my belief in the Creator was like an insurance policy I'd drafted to get me into heaven and away from eternal suffering; condemnation to eternal suffering being the standard punishment for those without unquestioning belief. Sadly, the premium—unquestioning belief—was never paid, so the policy was never in effect.

These contradictory beliefs about what the Creator is capable of, inevitably became evident in my life. How could I forgive myself for transgressions that I believed the Creator could not forgive? Which sinner among us can believe that the Creator has their back when It allows leukemia to strike out the lives of countless innocent babes? I doubt there is anyone who can, and this is why it's so important to develop a truer understanding of the nature of the Creator. The truer the understanding, the better the life.

Personal Gods

The question "Who or what is God?" is an ageless one. My purpose here is not to answer that question for you; it is to help you to see how your perception of the Creator (known by some as God, Allah, etc.) determines how you see yourself and, consequently, what meaning you ascribe to your life.

Let us suppose that we are all made in the image and likeness of the Creator. This may become a problem for you the moment you look in the mirror. When you see arms, legs, a face, and eyes, you may be fooled by seeing a god made in your image and likeness. Such a personal reality would hijack the notion of the true Creator as infinite and beyond categorical description, and would be accepted by your subconscious mind as a sure conclusion that it would then use to manage your life.

Moving on from considering yourself alone, there are such anthropomorphic (person-like) gods in the subconscious minds of billions of persons around the world, controlling their actions. These gods are no more than extensions of the personalities of those who have them roaming around their subconscious minds. Each of their imperfections, each of their foibles are magnified in their personified gods. All of these gods are, by definition, limited, capricious, dualistic—that is, hating some and loving others—and have many other characteristics that it is impossible, by definition, for the Creator to possess. The Creator is infinite and, as such, is indivisible and cannot be dualistic. Those believing in anthropomorphic gods do not recognize the unity of a singular Creator. When things are going well, they thank their gods for being so blessed; when they go badly, they curse gods that could allow such bad things to happen to good people.

Everyone, including one professing atheism, believes in a god. For some, it is the anthropomorphic god of their own making; for others it is the scientific method, nature, the universe, money, and so on. Few get to know the Creator. The question, "Do you believe in the Creator?" is not as important as "What do you believe about the Creator?" The latter is arguably the most important question you can ever ask yourself. Your answer will determine your perceived relationship to and with the Creator or the god you have substituted. It will help determine your self-image and the meaning you ascribe to your life.

Although you're made in the Creator's image and likeness, you must remember that the image you have of the Creator is from your personal perception of It, and is not the absolute truth about It. You cannot know the infinite. To know anything places limits on it and makes it finite.

Being created in the Creator's image and likeness, you share Its attributes. But, because those attributes are incorporeal and unknowable by your mind and five senses, you substitute the incorporeal and unknowable with something corporeal and knowable. As far as we know, there is no higher expression of life in the corporeal and knowable realms than humanity. So, it is little wonder that an inquiring mind would use the highest and best expression of life in those realms to represent the Creator's image and likeness.

When your self-image is consistent with the image and likeness of the Creator—infinitely good, eternal, and omniscient—you are much likelier to enjoy a life that is blessed. This is so because the enhanced self-image will lead you toward actions that align with your spiritual perfection. Put another way, as our photon from the previous chapter said, you create the illusion that suits you best. Seeing yourself as intelligent, healthful, and powerful will drive you toward actions that differ markedly from the actions you'd take if you saw yourself as stupid, unhealthy and impotent.

Such a self-image is neither developed overnight, nor is it likely ever to be fully developed. Nevertheless, it can be developed to a point by regularly apprehending your spiritual nature. This is largely done in meditation, but we will consider exactly how in more detail in a later chapter. For now, let's be satisfied that to see your image and likeness in the mirror as godly, you must look through what you possess (your body) to see your true self (spirit).

Interpreting Truth

Now, while the Creator is unable to be anything other than perfect, you have the freedom to express your spiritual perfection in the mind-body realms very imperfectly indeed. Such expression is often the direct opposite of any concept of godliness, but it is not a reflection of the Creator; it is not something for which you may blame the Creator, and it is no indication that the Creator is capable of creating or perceiving sin or evil.

A good explanation of this is given by the late spiritual teacher, Emmet Fox, who put it something like this: The 9th Symphony, as composed by Beethoven, is perfect. If played by a novice, however, you'd hardly recognize it as such. I'd even go so far as to say that the rendition of it would be sinful! The poor rendition would have absolutely nothing to do with Beethoven's perfect composition, and everything to do with the novice's inability to "live up to it," given their ignorance of how to do so. However, the more the novice learned how to play it as its true form, the more they'd *want* to play it as it ought to be played. The novice's answer to the question, "What do you know about Beethoven's 9th Symphony?" would be very different and significantly more incomplete than that of a maestro who is capable of conducting an orchestra that can follow the maestro's direction and deliver a performance close to the perfection that Beethoven imagined when composing the symphony.

To develop your understanding of this crucial point further, let's look at the same concept from another perspective. Your spirit-self perceives only perfection, while your mind and body selves can perceive imperfection. In truth (spirit), the imperfections don't exist; from a personal perception of reality (your mind and your body), they only *appear* to exist. In truth, three plus five always equals eight. In reality, you can make three plus five equal to, say, seven or nine. Perception is reality, so the mental and physical sufferings and joys you experience, while real, are not true (recognized or experienced in the spiritual realm). This, I believe, is the meaning of Maya as it is referred to in the Hindu and Buddhist traditions.

If every interpretation of a given situation, person, place, or thing was as black-and-white as basic mathematics, our problems would be few. The many shades of gray involved in first understanding and then interpreting life's written and unwritten rules, cultural nuances, and the like, are difficult enough. When we then add into the mix distinguishing between individuals' personal opinions and objective facts, interpreting correctly becomes all the more difficult.

These interpretations are affected by two of the things we'll examine in the following chapter: what you have faith in, and the complexes stored in your subconscious mind.

Because there are as many realities as there are persons capable of perceiving reality, no two persons perceive and, therefore, experience the world in exactly the same way. Dissimilar realities will often cause discordant relationships, from the sandpit in a children's playground to armed conflict between nations. The more precise cause of disharmony is the fragility of the personal ego, rather than the dissimilarity itself. Each person's ego places him or her at the center of their personal universe. Life is more harmonious when we always bear in mind that, no matter how errant, every personal reality (mind-body experience) is a descendent of the One Truth. As covered in chapter 7, *The Nature of Spirit*, we are one.

Suffice it to say, the more you are in tune with divine perfection, the more inclined you are to express it in your life. This is achieved by narrowing the gap between your personal reality and spiritual truth. The gap can be narrowed through meditation and using neuro·ADAPT·ive Programming.

The Purpose of Corporeal Life

So, the purpose of your corporeal life is to perfect your understanding of spirit so that you can create body-mind circumstances from the spiritual realm that are as close to the divine perfection of spirit as you can manage. There can be no greater meaning ascribed to your life than that of evolving infinite, eternal spirit into one of its manifold expressions through your own personality, to the best of your ability, in the full knowledge of who you are: a physical expression of consciousness, which is spirit.

The more you perfect your understanding of spirit and your relationship to and with spirit, the more capable you are of living up to your responsibility as a cocreator with the Creator. Your circumstances are brighter and are the inevitable effects of causes you purposely set in motion, from within, and not from without yourself. The remaining chapters of this book are all devoted to your developing this understanding and applying it to purposely create your fulfilling life.

The Problem of Knowing and Believing

The problem of knowing and believing arises when we assume knowledge of something when, in reality, all we have is a belief about that thing. We don't know a thing unless we can prove it for ourselves; everything else is belief. For instance, we assume the knowledge that the earth revolves around the sun, and that it spins on a tilted axis. We think we know what an axis is until we try to describe one. Our knowledge comes from trust in some authority telling us that this is the way it is, and we accept it without question.

We think we know that Paris is in France, and that France is in Europe, without ever having been there, because we have maps created by very clever persons, and because of the tales of those who have traveled there. We'd look rather foolish if we openly doubted this evidence—and so we don't. In fact, the thought of doing so never occurs to us, and yet, we can relate to the notion that if two people were told tales of a certain bakery on the *Rue de la Gare*, they might have different ideas about how the fresh baguettes might taste and how the buttery croissants might flake when torn apart. We only get a true personal knowledge from going to said bakery and experiencing it for ourselves.

Now, don't misunderstand me. I too buy into this convenience of *knowing* what I only believe. For the most part, not doing so would make life impossible. How could you function if you had to verify the authenticity of every precept, fact, and figure presented to you? However, when it comes to knowing the Creator while also being who you want to be, doing what you want to do, and getting what you want out of life, it is unwise to rely solely on the testimony of others. Mentors, coaches, and role models can lead you to the water, but you must drink it yourself to prove that it quenches *your* thirst. Yes, there is some risk involved; the water may be contaminated. But the risk cannot be avoided if you want to achieve your worthy ideal, instead of living vicariously through the ideals of others.

Not risking and simply accepting the testimony of others will likely have you believing (knowing) that you aren't good enough, smart enough, lucky enough, beautiful enough, wealthy enough, or deserving enough to live life on your own terms. It is also the case that many are coerced into living lives of continual struggle to present the façade that hides the psychological desperation they feel inside. But, it is to no avail. As within, so without. Their little secret is known by others. Their saving grace is that others suffer from the same malady and are only too willing to accept the lie, in a pact that has everyone else accepting theirs.

If, as mentioned previously, we are made in the image and likeness of the Creator, we ought to *know* of the Creator above *believing* in the Creator. This can be evidenced in the equality of the life circumstances of believers and nonbelievers. Since we cannot touch, taste, smell, hear, or see the Creator, and since thinking of the Creator constructs a god of limitation that cannot therefore *be* the Creator, how are we to *know* the Creator? Typically, this knowledge comes from trust in some authority telling us what the Creator is, which we accept without question. Such second-hand knowledge can only promote a belief in the Creator, rather than a true knowledge of the Creator. There is but one way to develop this true knowledge; the Creator must be experienced spiritually by stilling the body and quieting the mind. A belief in the Creator changes nothing; experiencing the Creator changes everything. This is the only way we can prove the Creator's existence for ourselves. Chapter 12 provides the tools by which you may develop a better knowledge of the Creator to most effectively apply the principles of neuro·ADAPT·ive Programming.

Your Fulfilling Life Action Assignment

1. What inherited beliefs about the Creator prevent you from fully expressing who you are?

2. An individual's theosophy is a statement of his or her spiritual philosophy. Write a description of your theosophy. Continue to refine it over time until it resonates perfectly with your spiritual beliefs. For example, an initial theosophy might be something like, "There is but one Creator, infinite and eternal, through which and from which all things are made. So, there is no Creator and the universe, but the Creator expressed as the universe and everything contained therein."

3. a. If you were the Creator, what one quality would you instill in every person?

    b. What are you going to do to ensure that this same quality is operating within you?

> *A belief in the Creator changes nothing; experiencing the Creator changes everything.*

CHAPTER NINE

Faith and Fear as Creative and Destructive Forces

Divine energy is always flowing through you. It permeates you, and you are inseparable from it. Even though you cannot be separated from this inexhaustible, eternal power, you can considerably reduce its flow through you by being ignorant of its existence or of how it works for good within you.

This cosmic power is spirit; it is the same power that creates the circumstances of your life. However, as you do not have the infinite capabilities of spirit, the availability of cosmic power is significantly more limited to you. There are two forces that affect the conversion of cosmic power to create the circumstances of your life. One, fear, is the opposite of the other, faith.

Placebos and Nocebos

Before we advance over unfamiliar ground about how faith and fear operate in our lives as creative and destructive forces, let us first consider commonplace examples from our lives.

> *While placebos do not contain an active element to affect outcomes, our faith in them does.*

A placebo is a substance like a saline solution or a sugar pill with no curative properties. The placebo effect is an actual curative effect achieved from the application or implied application of such a fake remedy. While placebos do not contain an active element to affect outcomes, our faith in them does. That faith can be so powerful that even fake surgeries have created placebo effects to "cure" patients of their conditions.

A nocebo is a substance without harmful properties. The nocebo effect is an actual harmful effect from the application or implied application of such a fake harmful agent. While nocebos do not contain harmful ingredients, our belief that they do is sufficient for the harmful effects to actually occur. Clinical trials using placebos have frequently had trialists taking the placebo and, by doing so, experiencing the side effects of the real drug. Their minds trick them into experiencing the side effects of the real drug. A chronic itching study published in *Allergy* in 2015 demonstrated how taking a harmless nocebo caused participants to imagine they were experiencing severe, chronic itching. The researchers noted the significant role that expectations and other psychological factors play in the condition of chronic itch patients.

The nocebo effect can be so powerful as to induce death. An example of this is one that killed an assistant working for the eighteenth-century Viennese medic, Erich Menninger von Lerchenthal. Students faked the young man's beheading by dropping a wet towel on the back of his neck and chopping an ax into a block of wood while he was blindfolded, and he died.

The nocebo effect underlies sinister practices like voodoo, witchcraft, and sorcery. More pertinent to creating a fulfilling life on purpose, it can also underlie more benign activities like hanging around negative people, accepting without question cultural beliefs that do not serve your best interests, and advertisements that play on your emotions. These include health ads that tell you how sick you might be, philanthropy ads that plead for your donation, and lifestyle ads that remind you of your unfulfilled ambitions. If you're not aware of the potential nocebo threats they pose, the subliminal messages they convey could become unconscious feelings that are stored in your subconscious, like fear, guilt, inferiority, and so on.

Cosmic Power: Your Creative Raw Material

In a sense, you are a conductor of cosmic power; it flows through you just as electricity flows through a copper wire. Typically, the flow of electricity through a copper wire is restricted by the resistance inherent in the copper wire while, at the same time, the flow is aided by the wire's conductivity.

You can see why resistance is inherent in copper wire when you imagine being pulled along a wooden floor while wearing rubber-soled shoes. The friction between the wood and the rubber slows down your movement along the floor. If you took off your shoes and were pulled along in your woolen socks, there'd be much less friction, and you'd flow along the floor much easier and much more quickly.

Your fears have a similar effect on you, as a conductor of cosmic power, as rubber shoes have on a wooden floor. Concepts and ideas that may improve your life are slowed down—sometimes so considerably, if your fears are great—that it makes the concepts and ideas unclear, and therefore unavailable to you. So, you remain stuck in the comfort zone of quiet desperation. Conversely, when you grow in faith, it's like taking off those rubber-soled shoes and sliding along the floor in your socks. Concepts and ideas flow to and through you at a rapid rate, and you can make significant strides toward your worthy ideal.

According to Your Faith

From this, it becomes apparent that the more faith and the less fear you have, the more effective your contributions in life will be. Because fear is the opposite of faith, as your faith grows, fear is automatically reduced. This should be self-evident in the same way that if right and left are opposites, the more you move to the right, the less you are to the left; and you are less to the left by the exact amount that you move to the right. Perfect faith is, therefore, the absence of fear. Is this state of being possible? If yes, and you achieved such a state, you'd no longer have any resistance to cosmic power. It would flow through you, unrestricted.

With such faith, you could create an extraordinary, fulfilling life of meaning and purpose. This kind of faith is like becoming a superconductor (which is a conductor that has zero resistance, and, as such, allows the full capacity of available energy to pass through it). When faith is looked at in this way, the adage, "According to your faith be it unto you" can be treated like precise logic, rather than mystical fancy. A quantum leap in personal power is attained not by doing more but, in a sense, by doing less; and that is to "let go and let God." While this is an oft-quoted aphorism, it is seldom accompanied by an explanation of *how* you can do it. There is more to it than being inactive and hoping for divine intervention; precise instructions on how you can let go and let God are provided in the final act of the neuro·ADAPT·ive Programming process in chapter 12.

Before we get there, let's take a closer look at what faith is. A better understanding of faith is the first step in developing faith. The development of faith will enable a freer flow of cosmic power, which will, in turn, increase your personal power. This is where the quantum leap begins.

The Power of F.A.I.T.H.

Faith is a subject that is much talked of, but little understood. The first thing to be sure of is that everyone has faith, and that each person's faith is undeniable. You absolutely, without doubt, create according to your faith. The two big questions you need to ask are, "Faith in what?" and, "Is faith helping or hindering you?"

It is helpful to see faith as a scale in degrees of certainty about an outcome. It runs from wishing to hoping, through believing, expecting, and knowing that an outcome will occur. If you lived in a home with running water and wanted a glass of water, you'd have a very high degree of certainty—call it knowing—that you could get one. On the other hand, if you've suffered a life of just getting by, your degree of certainty about becoming wealthy may be as low as wishing or hoping.

Now, here is my definition of faith:

Feelings Accepted In The Heart

This definition provides the complete explanation for why we sometimes self-sabotage; why bad things happen to good people; why *good* things happen to *bad* people; why the rich get richer while the poor get poorer; and why an individual may go from rags to riches, then back to rags again.

"Heart" is the name the ancients used for what is now more commonly called the subconscious or unconscious mind.

> For as he thinketh in his heart, so is he.
> **—Proverbs 23:7**

Your subconscious beliefs (and not whether you are good or bad) determine the circumstances of your life.

Freud's experience from his clinical practice caused him to conclude that the subconscious mind has mental processes that are inaccessible to the conscious mind, but that still influence our conscious judgments, feelings, and behaviors.

Carl Jung demonstrated how future behavior is determined by the aspirations and repressed memories stored in the subconscious mind. In outlining the effects of these positive and negative factors, he coined the term *complex*. A complex is a collection of factors—thoughts, feelings, attitudes, and memories—stored in the subconscious, which Jung said drives our behavior around a single concept. For instance, a person may have a complex around the concept of relationships formed from the thoughts, feelings, attitudes, and memories of childhood abuse, school bullying, poor parenting, and so on.

The complex resulting from these factors may cause an individual to self-sabotage present-day relationships, in spite of a conscious desire for more fulfilling relationships. The factors attached to a relationship complex may include thoughts of revenge and suicide, feelings of inferiority and bitterness, and attitudes of hard-

> *Freud's experience from his clinical practice caused him to conclude that the subconscious mind has mental processes that are inaccessible to the conscious mind, but that still influence our conscious judgments, feelings, and behaviors.*

heartedness and aloofness. These are, of course, just a few examples from a large pool of thoughts, feelings and attitudes. The greater the number of factors attached to the complex, the greater its influence on the individual.

A complex is like a resistor in an electrical circuit that restricts the flow of electricity through a system. Therefore, a complex restricts the flow of cosmic energy through you, preventing you from comprehending the world as it really is. You will recall from chapter 5 that fear is an acronym for Future Evil Already Realized. Well, a complex is an example of the realization of precisely this. Because the future doesn't exist, the fear is, strictly speaking, unreal. It is consistent with the other fear acronym we encountered in chapter 5: False Evidence Appearing Real. So, a complex around relationships might create a future evil already realized—FEAR—of being hurt by a prospective partner. A complex around self-esteem might create a fear of your new venture failing. In this way, what you fear becomes a self-fulfilling prophecy. Complexes are neutralized by spiritually improving your self-image, as we discovered in chapter 7. Employing neuro·ADAPT·ive Programming will aid this process.

It is notable that ancient religious wisdom agrees with modern-day psychology. The Buddhist tradition comments on the concept of *ālaya-vijñāna* (storehouse consciousness), in which previous experiences are lodged in the *ālaya-vijñāna* to influence future experiences. Hinduism puts forward the idea of Sanskaras, which are past impressions, unconscious to the individual, that influence the individual's future behavior. And, from the Judeo-Christian tradition, we find advice such as:

Keep your heart with all diligence,
for out of it springs the issues of life.
— Proverbs 4:23

The key to faith, and to getting what you want, is to hold what you want with a *high degree of certainty*, regardless of what your current circumstances appear to be. Doing so is one of the mechanisms for invoking the law of attraction. In truth, you do this all the time anyway, but not always intentionally. The key is to always be intentional; when you don't have intentional faith, you'll often attract people, experiences, feelings, and circumstances you don't want into your life.

During cold season, do you expect to get a cold or flu? Do you carry the fear of ill-health, or losing your job, being unloved, not having enough money, failing in business, not being good enough, not being smart enough, and so on? When you hold these fears, they become expectations lodged in your subconscious mind, so even when you consciously want their opposites, your subconscious mind only delivers on that which you have placed your faith in. This is why I confidently say that all faith is undeniable and that the sage advice, "According to your faith, be it unto you," is precise logic.

There are three important components of faith: Action, Conviction, and Expectation, or ACE. When you have faith in something—even when it is misplaced faith—you act with the conviction of one expecting a certain outcome. So, faith without works—outcomes—is dead; in fact, stillborn. Works automatically flow from faith. However, works produced without an understanding of faith may be misguided. Faith is cause, while works are effects; the latter *must* proceed from the former—it is a universal principle. Therefore, your works come from what you truly have faith in, and these works are from the feelings that have been accepted in the heart.

Life is a self-fulfilling prophecy.

Developing Faith

You have already begun the process of developing faith by merely having an accurate and workable definition thereof:

Feelings Accepted In The Heart

Workable means that the definition is clear and that it has specific components—your actions, convictions, and expectations—that you can use as standards to compare where you are with where you'd like to be. A mechanic may do the same with the oil filter of a car they are working on, by comparing it with the standard filter for the make and model. In doing so, they can make a correct decision about whether or not to replace the filter. For instance, the standard against which they make the comparison (a fully functioning oil filter) is not covered in grease. If the one they are working on is, they may wish to change it.

Having an accurate and workable definition is just the beginning.

The emotions experienced in a life of abusive relationships can become, and are most likely to become, lodged in the heart (subconscious mind) as negative feelings toward developing intimate relationships. So, while a person with this experience may express a conscious desire to develop more loving relationships, the outcome (works) is often more of the same. It is so by the law of attraction. The feelings accepted in the heart of this person are inconsistent with their expressed desire; as within, so without. So, their professed faith is incongruent with their true faith.

To change what's in your heart, you have to work on ACE to develop your faith.

Action

The action required is that of acting as if you cannot fail, regardless of evidence to the contrary. This is the same wisdom that is behind Jesus's advice to believe that you have already received whatever you ask for in prayer, and in so doing, it will be yours.

For example, Eleanor leaves a high-paying corporate executive position to fulfill a lifetime ambition of owning her own business. She opens the doors three weeks before the most severe economic recession in thirty-four years. Orders are plummeting. Eleanor starts to listen to the economic news far more frequently than she ever did before. After all, her knowing up-to-the-minute economic conditions is in her business's interest. The bleaker the news, the more hopeless Eleanor's personal outlook, and the deeper her despair.

What Eleanor has done, like most, is to place her faith in external circumstances rather than in increasing her ability to convert, more efficiently, the cosmic power that is ceaselessly coming her way. Her faith, expressed as fear, is in economic conditions. The feelings associated with this fear are transmitted to the subconscious mind, which delivers on Eleanor's faith. It has to; it cannot do anything else. It operates according to laws, and the laws it bows to are the laws of creation: the laws of attraction and repulsion, the law of karma, and the law of polarity (see chapter 10 for more about these laws). The subconscious mind only knows how to say yes to anything you ask for with faith, even if that faith is unintentionally misplaced and detrimental to you.

What we are seeing here is an example of how the notions lodged in our subconscious mind affect our lives in accordance with Freud's clinical experience, Jung's complex theory, and the findings of the various religious traditions we previously discussed.

What Eleanor needs to do is hold fast to her beliefs and act according to them. In seeing the outcome she wants, Eleanor could ignore the reported doom and gloom, and act as if success is inevitable. She might devise a more targeted sales campaign, upgrade the quality and quantity of employee training, provide a better customer experience, and maintain, rather than cut, her marketing budget. If Eleanor also used the practices I gave to one of my clients in chapter 7, she'd allow the providence of spirit to guide the circumstances of her life according to her faith, without any discernible changed activity in her body-mind realms.

These were:

- The creation of a mantra that best expressed what she really wanted;
- A visualization of what her life would look like when she got it;
- Combining the mantra and visualization as a prayer;
- Taking this prayer into contemplative meditation;
- And lastly, going into silent meditation in which this prayer would work at the spiritual level

I can personally corroborate the fidelity of acting as if you cannot fail. In a former capacity as a salesperson, I was given, unaware, a territory that several predecessors had failed to succeed in. I was very excited about my new position and was determined to succeed. Failing was not an option, though not from any sense of bravado; the thought simply didn't enter my mind. Needless to say, I succeeded greatly where others had failed. I was too new to be influenced by the sales force's collective programming that no one could succeed in *that* territory.

My success earned me a promotion to lead a team of twelve sales managers. During that time, I saw the "acting as if..." principle work time and again. New team members succeeded despite other people's negative programming about how the territory would work out for them, or anyone else it might be assigned to.

Furthermore, a 2009 study sponsored by the Kauffman Foundation discovered that over 50 percent of the *Fortune 500* companies from that year had been launched when the economy was in decline or recession. Other successful recession start-ups include Apple Inc., Burger King, CNN, General Electric, General Motors, IBM (founded as the Tabulating Machine Company), Microsoft, and the Walt Disney Company.

Conviction

When you are convinced, there is no room for doubt. Doubt breeds fear, whereas conviction breeds faith.

While many couples are totally comfortable being in a relationship together without allowing the notion of marriage to affect their happiness one way or another, I once knew a couple (let's call them Bill and Margaret), for whom that was not the case.

They dated for years and lived together most of that time, but were jittery about getting married. They were faithful to each other, but a lack of trust prevented them from completely committing themselves to each other. Arguments were a regular feature of their life together.

One day, out of the blue, Bill proposed to Margaret. After considering the proposal for several weeks, Margaret finally accepted. Would you know it, from that moment on and throughout their marriage, the level of trust shot through the roof, while arguments fell through the floor. Once they were convicted (and I use the word advisedly) to a lifelong partnership, the vacuum of doubt vanished. In its place was certainty.

Expectation

Emotion is an extremely important component of expectation. Emotions are the conduit along which your desires—good, bad, ugly, advertent, or inadvertent—are transported to the subconscious and lodged there as feelings. Expecting things to turn out badly will have the associated negative emotions (resentment, depression) that fuel fear and increase your resistance to cosmic power. Expecting things to turn out well will have the associated positive emotions (joy, gratitude) that fuel faith and increase your conductivity of cosmic power.

Spend just a little time contemplating the three components of faith, and it will be quickly apparent how each interacts with the other to either empower or disempower you. ACE is not a formula for removing every adversity from your life. There is no such formula. Developing the consciousness for divine providence to guide your life can happen quickly, but may also take years. Regardless of your timeline, the incremental gains along the way are certainly worth the time and effort. Life is guaranteed to come with thorns, so it's better to be a rose than a prickly weed.

Making the Quantum Leap

Remember, the flow rate of cosmic power comes from the interplay between your faith and your fear. By moving toward the former, you increase conductivity; and by moving toward the latter, you increase resistance. What, then, can be done to unleash a quantum leap in faith?

> *Life is guaranteed to come with thorns, so it's better to be a rose than a prickly weed.*

Most people believe that increasing their faith brings them closer to knowing the Creator—Truth. Not so, precisely. Faith in the Creator is developed by getting to know the Creator; just as faith in a coworker's competence is developed by familiarity with their work.

There are as many realities as there are persons to perceive them; and yet, there is but One Truth—one cosmic power, the Creator. Your ability to perceive reality as pure truth would require the complete absence of resistance to cosmic power. As discussed earlier in the chapter, achieving this requires total faith, which is automatically coupled with the total absence of fear.

Your interface with cosmic power is your mind. Therefore, you may grow your faith by knowing and developing your mind. Psychologists see the mind as a set of cognitive faculties: emotions, imagination, intuition, memory, perception, reason, thinking, and will.

Developing your capacities within each of the faculties can be the catalyst for that elusive quantum leap. Make no mistake; the difference between the average person and geniuses like Einstein and da Vinci can be explained exclusively in how these faculties are used.

For now, let us be satisfied with a hypothetical, generic example of the proper use of the mind and how all of these cognitive faculties work together. Suppose you get an *intuitive* hunch and apply your *will* to focus on that hunch until your *imagination* is fired. What you imagine, with the continued application of will, may morph into a series of related and progressive *thoughts*—each building on your *memory* of those preceding it—that form into an idea. Before long, your idea crystalizes into a concept, which you *perceive* from differing perspectives to perfect the initial concept. The excitement you feel about being on the cusp of something quite special ignites more positive *emotions* that drive you on without stress but, instead, the calm assurance that you've got this and are fully capable of taking it from here. The subconscious mind responds in kind, and the developing concept leads to a hypothesis which, by a process of inductive *reasoning*, you refine into a theory, formula, model, prototype, or distinction of some sort, which is directly applicable in the world for the benefit of many.

So, another worthy ideal becomes reality, and the ceaseless motion of the evolutionary wheel turns once more.

Your Fulfilling Life Action Assignment

1. a. On a scale of 1 to10, with 10 being high, how fearful are you of pursuing your worthy ideal?

    b. What three things can you do to reduce your level of fear? One example is to begin the day by reading something motivational or inspirational. Another is to review the positive attributes that are taking you toward your worthy ideal, every morning and every night.

2. What three things will you commit to doing to increase your faith?

3. Think of a time when you had to overcome fear to accomplish something. Write yourself a letter explaining what the task was, what you were afraid of, and how you overcame the fear. Continue the letter by explaining how you felt once you had achieved the task. Mail the letter to yourself. When you receive it, set aside some time to read it. Make a note of the lessons you can apply from your previous experience in pursuit of your worthy ideal.

CHAPTER TEN

The Laws of Creation

The Process of Creation

No one can refrain from cocreating. The resolution for cocreation was written, ratified, signed, and sealed long before records began. Every time you think with a degree of conviction, you set in motion the process of creating something. The best you can do, then, is to become the most effective cocreator you are capable of being.

The process of creation begins with an idea. Everything required to realize an idea is attracted to that idea. The subconscious mind is the medium through which every required component is attracted to you. Your vision is the catalyst for the idea (or worthy ideal); the resources to make it happen are the means. Your creative energy around the idea enables or prevents, attracts or repels its realization.

During the neuro·ADAPT·ive Programming process, you will be harnessing your creative energy and directing it toward achieving your fulfilling life.

How Your Thoughts Cause Outcomes

A significant difference between causes and effects is that causes are eternal and infinite, while effects are temporal and finite; they have a shelf life. So, as a cocreator, you have an unlimited source of ideas (let's call them thoughts) to choose from, but once those ideas are manifested as things—money, relationships, businesses, jobs—they cannot last forever. Furthermore, your five senses are incapable of comprehending most of what is around you. To say that what you see is the tip of the iceberg would be a monumental understatement:

"There are invisible forces all around us. What we call matter is condensed energy. The invisible world is pure energy. Our tendency is to accept as reality what we see. When we open our eyes, we think we are seeing the whole world out there. But what has become clear in the last few centuries, is that when we look at the electromagnetic spectrum, we are capable of seeing only a tiny portion of what we call visible light.

"The next time you think, 'seeing is believing,' think again! Your eyes can only perceive 4 percent of the total information that rides on the electromagnetic spectrum. Everything else passing around and through your body is completely invisible to you. You are seeing just a narrow window of what is happening. Imagine what you're missing!"

—Dr. Jussi Eerikäinen, author, ***Transforming Vibes, Transforming Lives***

Much of the 96 percent of the universe you cannot see is referred to by cosmologists as *dark matter* or *dark energy*. It is perhaps an unfortunate term. While it refers to unseen substance, it does *not* imply dark thoughts or negative energy in any sense. Your job as a cocreator is to bring what exists as *invisible* forms into *visible* forms. These forms will be the circumstances of your life. When you engage the four forces of creation described in this chapter, imagine that you are changing the vibrational frequency of dark matter into more condensed forms that you can see, and what you then see is what you've manifested. Everything that you can possibly desire already exists; your job is to train your mind to manifest the good you desire. This is the entire purpose of neuro·ADAPT·ive Programming.

The Attractive Force

The first thing I'd like to do in discussing this force is to declare my belief in its efficacy. The second thing I'd like to do is to expose the nonsense in much of what has been said about the law of attraction in recent decades.

Many persons talk of it as though all you need to do is close your eyes, settle down in a quiet place, and pull everything that you want from life toward you by visualization alone. Sure, that is a recipe for *feeling great*, but it lacks sufficient substance for *becoming great*. The law of attraction is not a silver bullet that provides instant remedies for long-standing problems; practicing the law provides an opportunity for the spiritual growth required to achieve your worthy ideal. You cannot ignore Emerson's law of compensation, which states that we are compensated according to our contribution. This is a restatement of the law of sowing and reaping, so you're going to have to take some everyday actions that contribute to the betterment of others to get what you want.

The late spiritual teacher Emmet Fox described character as "a bundle of habits with a customary outlook."

> *The law of attraction is not a silver bullet that provides instant remedies for long-standing problems;*

Growth is the improvement of your character to form a better, more effective outlook that takes you toward achieving your worthy ideal. To improve character, you must change your way of thinking. Another way of putting this is that your character is a reflection of your mind's activity—a changed character doesn't happen by listening to guided meditations, or chanting affirmations, alone. The brilliance of these spiritual tools, as I like to call them, is that they make your mind more fertile for the necessary changes to take root.

If a farmer were to plant his crops without spreading fertilizer, he'd soon find them wanting for the lack of it. The addition of fertilizer provides enhanced conditions for better growth, so you need to fertilize your mind to protect against the negative thoughts that haunt it. By all means, do so with positive meditations and affirmations to create a fertile mental environment in which you can work on changing your way of thinking to improve your character. Always remember: the seeds are what is in your subconscious mind; the quality of the seeds is affected by the complexes held there; what you think about is the sowing of the seeds; and, what you harvest is evident in the circumstances of your life.

The law of attraction is a consequence of the law of vibration (of energy), which is a measurable physical quantity. It may be defined as an attractive force within the universe, which draws like energies together.

Einstein's equation $E = MC^2$ proves the convertibility of matter into energy. The equation is the basis of the principle behind nuclear fission, in which the nucleus of an atom is split into smaller parts, releasing masses of energy. The equation is also the scientific equivalent of modern-day mystic Darryl Anka's revelation that (according to him) was channeled through him by a multidimensional being known to him as Bashar:

Everything is here and now, but in various states of visibility and invisibility depending upon the frequency that you are operating on, and that means the belief system, the definitions that you buy into most strongly.... Everything is energy and that's all there is to it. Match the frequency with the reality you want and you cannot help but get that reality. It can be no other way. This is physics.

If thoughts exist (and they do), they must be energy. So, positive thoughts are attractors for positive experiences and negative thoughts are attractors for negative experiences. You are the attractor and, therefore, the law of attraction works best in your favor when you raise your consciousness to vibrate in harmony with the circumstances you want to attract, rather than by simply visualizing those circumstances.

The Repulsive Force

There is ample evidence that opposites attract just as well as likes attract. If you bring together two magnets at their north poles (likes), they will repel each other. This is like two alpha wolves clashing. However, bringing together the north pole of one magnet with the south pole of another (opposites) causes them to attract each other. This is like a type A personality being in a harmonious relationship with a type B personality; bringing the likes of two south poles together again causes repulsion.

Without the law of repulsion, planets would not remain in orbit and atoms would collapse, with their electrons imploding into their nuclei. You can see evidence of the principle of opposites attracting in relationships of all kinds: romantic, business, sporting...some of the best teams in social, business, and sporting relationships are composed of widely diverse personalities. Such teams are able to see opportunities and challenges from a broader spectrum of perspectives, thereby creating better solutions.

The Polar Forces

Polarity is another cosmic law. It has, or expresses, two opposite tendencies, or forces. It is important to understand that while these tendencies or forces are opposites, they are not *opposing*; in fact, they are complementary: a lock and a key, a hole and a peg, a female and a male, a pitcher and a catcher, an electron and a proton. Everything is created from two opposite yet complementary things. For example, a child is the product of a union between a man and a woman.

The most important polarity with which this book is concerned is that of your conscious and subconscious minds. Whenever your conscious mind imagines, dreams, or thinks, with sufficient faith and emotion, it impresses those imaginings, dreams, or thoughts upon the subconscious mind to produce an outcome: a book, a business, a spouse, a family, poverty, riches, illness, health...

Your conscious thoughts comingle with and stir up, so to speak, your subconscious mind, which changes the vibrational frequency of cosmic energy so that the vibrational rate becomes condensed enough to crystalize into an energy which is compact enough for your conscious mind and five senses to perceive as being the circumstances of your life.

The Karmic Force

While many people view karma as the law of retribution, it really refers to the effects set in motion by causes you initiate. Those causes may, of course, have beneficial as well as retributive repercussions; you reap what you sow. For all intents and purposes, then, karma is the law of cause and effect. There is no such thing as a cause without an effect, and an effect is always consistent with its cause: acorns will always produce oak trees, and never apple trees. This is why "you will know them [i.e., people] by their fruits" (Matt. 7:16).

Secondary Causes (or Primary Effects)

Conventional wisdom will tell you that for every cause, there is an effect; and so there is. Generally speaking, if you overeat empty carbs and don't exercise, you'll gain fat cells and weight; spend more than you earn, and you'll deplete financial resources; overdraw the emotional bank account you have with a significant other, and that relationship will decline; and so on. However, these causes, and any others that can be observed within the universe, are secondary, which means that they, themselves, are caused by something else. They, too, are effects. These effects are primary effects because they have knock-on effects. For example, texting while driving may be regarded as the primary effect of a car crash. There are several secondary effects in between the texting and the crash, like slamming on the brakes, swerving the steering wheel, and screaming some expletives. What initiates the primary effect is a thought, or a way of thinking. Your way of thinking creates a state of being, which determines your behaviors; behaviors in turn create habits, which produce the circumstances of your life.

If you apply this chain of causality to the car crash, you

will see that thinking is what started the chain in motion. The distracted driver must have had the thought to text someone. If their typical way of thinking was frenzied, they would be more likely to behave impatiently. That impatience develops the habit of multitasking, even at inappropriate times. In this case, it has culminated in the car crash—the current circumstances of the driver's life.

Putting the Cart Before the Horse

Let's refer back to the statistic which is re-popularized every New Year: ninety-two percent of people who make New Year's resolutions fail to keep them. Surely, this is evidence of something amiss—and in a big way. The crux is that we need to change our thinking for material changes to stick.

The most popular diet in the world is the yo-yo diet. It's the one where you start a diet program, lose some weight, and before you know it, there's a slice of pizza—or some other forbidden fruit—sliding down your throat and tickling your esophagus, before landing in your stomach. Of course, you then gain back whatever weight you lost. Eventually, you decide this program just doesn't work, so you move onto the next one and the yo-yo pattern is repeated.

Have you ever wondered why one-third of lottery jackpot winners declare bankruptcy (according to the Certified Financial Planner Board of Standards)? The obvious (though not best) answer is that they need better financial advice and planning. However, as with dieting, dating, business, and anything else you care to mention, the best answer is that many of them did not have the mindset that would allow them to keep hold of the money. The most important bequest you can leave your children

> *Have you ever wondered why one-third of lottery jackpot winners declare bankruptcy*

is not the money and assets you've accumulated, but the way of thinking that enabled you to do so, while enjoying a fulfilling life on purpose. This is the treasure that is said to be stored in heaven (your consciousness) where moths and rust cannot destroy it, and thieves cannot break in and steal it.

Attempting to create changes in your life by directly affecting your material circumstances, is an effort at manipulating primary effects. A better approach is to change how you think about the outcomes you want.

Readjusting the Horse and Cart

Primary Causes

The conclusion you can draw from all of these examples, then, is that there is no such thing as a physical cause. The universe was created which, by definition, makes it an effect. The most outstanding and convincing proof of this is that everything in the physical world that has been created by humans, was first a mental activity. Concepts, ideas, thoughts, imagination—these lead to physical effects, but behind those mental activities is your state of being, which is determined by your subconscious mind. It is in the subconscious (spiritual) realm where the mental activity you engage in is determined and is, therefore, the source of primary causes. So, when René Descartes said, "I think; therefore, I am," he didn't get to the root of causality—the spiritual realm. Had he done so, he'd have said, "I am; therefore, I think." That is, he'd have put cause *before* effect instead of vice versa. The true "I am" is the spiritual you, not the physical you.

The reason I've emphasized this point is to instill in you the importance of going to the root of cause and effect to initiate changes that will improve your life. It is always your subconscious state of being, in the form of the complexes hidden there, that drives your behaviors to create the circumstances of your life. Remember, though, there is one force that can change your subconscious programming: your conscious mind. By imprinting new patterns of mental activity on your subconscious mind with heightened emotions in faith, you can change your subconscious state of being. You will be shown how to do this using neuro·ADAPT·ive Programming; it will allow you to initiate more beneficial causes to purposely create your fulfilling life.

A Harmonious Arrangement

While we can discuss the forces of creation as separate entities in principle, they are, in practice, inseparable functions of the law of creation. Let's look at the orbit of a planet to show you what I mean.

Polarity

The gravitational forces of the sun, and other planets in the solar system, combine with the opposing force of the planet in question's momentum to hold it in orbit.

Attraction

Gravity is also the attractive force acting upon the planet, which would pull it into its sun if it were a force in isolation.

Repulsion

The planet's momentum acts as a repulsive force which, if acting in isolation, would propel the planet out of its orbit.

Karma

You cannot argue that, with a planet, what goes around, comes around.

In chapter 12 you will learn how to put all the forces of creation together to create your own fulfilling life.

Your Fulfilling Life Action Assignment

1. a. You've created your current circumstances by your dominant thoughts, influenced by what is stored in your subconscious mind. Identify one dominant thought that might be contributing to any current circumstances you do not care for.

    b. Trusting your intuition, where do you imagine this belief may have come from?

    c. If the source is a person (or persons), mentally forgive them—if you believe forgiveness is appropriate.

    d. Replace the belief with one that better serves your purpose.

2. The idea of the self-made person is romantic fiction. What opposite and complementary skills do you need to attract by way of other people, in order to manifest your worthy ideal?

3. We learned in this chapter that Emmet Fox called character a bundle of habits with a customary outlook. So, a change in habits will cause a change in character, which will, in turn, cause a change in outlook. With this in mind, identify the negative habit that, if changed, would give you the biggest push towards creating your fulfilling life. What new positive habit are you going to replace it with?

CHAPTER ELEVEN

neuro·ADAPT·ive Programming—Preparation

Embrace the Power

Realizing that you are a creature with the privilege and responsibility for cocreation with the Creator, allows you to embrace the power within you to create the most rewarding life you are capable of.

The meaning you ascribe to your life will come from the ideals you pursue in life, and those ideals will come from the causes you think into being. You are a finite expression of the Creator, and this is the source of your power.

"We were born to make manifest the glory of God within us.

It's not just in some of us; it's in everyone."

—**Marianne Williamson**

The greater your capacity to express creator-like qualities such as beauty, forgiveness, love, and truth, the clearer will be your mission, the more meaning you will derive from life, and consequently, the more fulfillment you will

> *The meaning you ascribe to your life will come from the ideals you pursue in life, and those ideals will come from the causes you think into being.*

experience. By developing these creator-like qualities, you increase your receptivity to the cosmic power discussed in chapter 8 and increase your personal power.

Spiritual practices like meditation, visualization, contemplation, and prayer are fantastic ways to improve the causes you set in motion. These practices positively influence the faculties of the mind: emotions, imagination, intuition, memory, perception, reason, thinking, and will. As we have discussed, improving these faculties increases faith and decreases fear. These movements of faith and fear increase your capacity to use cosmic power to be more effective in your life.

When you work on spiritual causes, instead of trying to manipulate worldly effects and occasionally stumbling upon success, you control your blueprint for success. In this way, success becomes an inevitable and repeatable consequence of cause and effect. It has to be inevitable and repeatable because the subconscious mind knows but one answer, "*yes*," to all requests—both helpful or harmful—about which it believes you are sincere.

Perfection Is Not Required

Every model of the universe is incomplete, each being an approximation of universal truth, rather than the truth itself. In spite of their flaws, the predictive abilities of scientific models are increasingly impressive. This is great news for you and me; we don't have to have a complete understanding of everything we do to live effective, productive lives. If we don't fully comprehend the laws governing cocreation, we are not precluded from using them to create fulfilling lives.

Introduction to neuro·ADAPT·ive Programming

Put simply, neuro·ADAPT·ive Programming enables you to reduce the gap between your personal reality and spiritual truth. As with scientific models, you don't have to completely understand the mechanics of neuro·ADAPT·ive Programming to successfully transform your life by using it. By now, you'll know the difference between doing so and not, is F.A.I.T.H.

If you really pay attention, you'll notice that your personal reality comes from your thinking. However, you probably also allow your experiences and the culture you are part of to affect your thinking. So, what you have is material circumstances influencing how you think. From the previous chapter you'll realize that this is an example of putting the cart before the horse—it is also what Eleanor from chapter 8 was doing when she allowed poor economic conditions to determine how she thought about the prospects of her business. Continually allowing circumstances to negatively affect your thinking is how the cycle of despair persists for you. The cycle is broken only when you stop reacting to external stimuli and, instead, turn to the meaning you want for your life, for guidance.

To know what your personal reality is, simply look at your circumstances: the quality of your health, relationships, career satisfaction, finances, and so on. None of these are the way they are by accident, luck, providence, or mistake: your thinking makes them so. It is worth repeating here that a change in circumstances requires a change in thinking.

Ultimate truth holds infinite possibilities. So, you can have from life whatever your mind can conjure with sufficient desire and faith. A gap between your reality

Creating a Fulfilling Life Through Spiritual Growth

(circumstances) and truth (your ideal) exists when there is something that you want from life but do not have. Realities are the effects of your thinking, and your subconscious state of being is the cause of how you think. To change effects, you need only change the causes of those effects. If a farmer wants to harvest wheat instead of corn, he must stop planting corn seeds and start planting wheat seeds.

Most of us impact the greatest number of people through our work. When we are engaged in work we do not care for, we are uninspired. However, when we do work we love, we are inspired, the origin of which is *in spirit*. Spirit is for expansion. This is evident in the expanding universe we inhabit and the continued evolution of everything within it.

neuro·ADAPT·ive Programming is designed to help you live a fulfilling life on purpose. Living life in this way is how you narrow the gap between your personal reality, evidenced by your present circumstances, and your truth, which is your desired circumstances. The closer they match, the more peace you will enjoy. If ever they match completely, you will experience a peace of mind more valuable than any material gain from worldly success you could ever imagine.

Applying the principles of neuro·ADAPT·ive Programming is the path away from the cycle of despair.

Independent studies have shown that under certain conditions—hypnosis, for example—the subconscious mind not only has perfect recall but also is capable of providing facts about future events, which have been proven correct when that future becomes the present. While not an exercise in hypnosis, this is the power that neuro·ADAPT·ive Programming exploits to transform your

> *Even your indecision is a decision not to decide, which carries a consequence. So, let's consider what it is we ought to decide on.*

ambitions from an uncertain future, there and then, to a concrete realization, here and now.

How to Use neuro·ADAPT·ive Programming

Everything begins with a decision and every decision has a consequence. Even your indecision is a decision *not* to decide, which carries a consequence. So, let's consider what it is we ought to decide on.

While neuro·ADAPT·ive Programming can be successfully used to create a singular thing like a car, a relationship, or a job, I want to encourage you to use it for creating your ideal lifestyle around a worthy ideal. Doing so will allow you to create the fullest expression of your life, as it sets up the causes you need in order to produce only the effects that you want in your life. This does not mean that you will be completely inoculated against life's challenges; you don't have perfect knowledge, or perfect command of the forces you will use to create your ideal lifestyle. However, using this approach gives you an opportunity to get more than any singular item you desire. It offers the chance to also create great relationships, a fulfilling vocation...the entire package. It is the pursuit and realization of the truth that sets you free.

There Goes the Baby With the Bathwater

What I'm about to share tends to be the most difficult step for my coaching clients; it requires a complete shedding of who you believe yourself to be. You are temporarily throwing out the baby with the bathwater. You need to do this to ensure that the baby in the bathtub is actual your own! Cuckoos lay their eggs in another bird's nest. The cuckoo offspring hatch early and push out the eggs from the sitting bird's nest, killing off its true offspring and ensuring its own survival.

Like it or not, you've unknowingly incubated and raised concepts, ideas, rules, and dogmas that are not your own offspring. Like the cuckoo, they have hatched early, ousting the ideas you *did* give birth to. Because of your oblivion, you've accepted the impostors as your own. Even now, you nurture them, feed them, and defend them; some with your very life. And yet, if you could see them for what they are, you'd toss them from your nest. This is your chance to do so. Take it!

Examining the preconceived ideas that you have about yourself, and the world may take some time and a lot of courage.

Don't rush it.

Allow it to unfurl.

This is not a race.

You're creating the life of your dreams.

Give it the time it warrants.

You must forget that you're a tinker, tailor, soldier, or sailor, a rich person, poor person, beggar or thief, a doctor, lawyer or union chief. You are not single, you are not married, you are neither old nor young. Everything must be set aside. Otherwise, you may create a better life, but it won't be the life of your dreams. Remember, if these identities are truly your own, they'll be proceeding forward with you. On the other hand, if they are cuckoos, you have some serious and potentially painful decisions to make.

In this process, you may find it helpful to jot down some notes. I highly recommend using a pad and pen (electronic, if you prefer). Draw two vertical lines down the page, so that they divide it into thirds. On the left-hand side, note all of the things you want to be, but believe you can't; all the things you'd love to do, but believe you can't; all the things you'd love to have, but believe you can't. In the center pane, note the reasons you believe you can't be, do, and have these things. Then, on the right-hand side, make a note of where the beliefs came from: your parents, friends, church, your country, a club you belong to. Use as many sheets of the pad as necessary to complete a thorough examination.

Doing this thoroughly takes sincere introspection. Sometimes, you have to study a cuckoo long and hard before you recognize it as such. There are no cuckoo-identifying magic pills—I'd be selling them if there were.

Designing Your Lifestyle

The next thing you must do, is determine how you would like to live. You are here, on earth, in a body through which you sense the world about you. There is nothing gained by denying that your life is expressed through the use of your body. Your body and the world through which it moves are the effects of spiritual causes, as we discussed earlier. Your spiritual nature causes your physical world; it does so either on purpose or by default. You must live with the circumstances you create. Why, if it is within your power, would you not create enjoyable, harmonious conditions for yourself and for others where you can? You either think it's impossible, or you believe it's possible but you don't know how. The neuro·ADAPT·ive Programming process can be your how.

When considering the lifestyle you want to lead, it is best to imagine the emotions you would like to feel and then consider what experiences you want that would produce those emotions. What I'm encouraging you to do, is to really get in touch with your uniqueness. Just like a corporation has a unique value proposition (UVP) to distinguish itself from competitors, you have a uniquely valuable persona. The basis of your UVP is your personality. Individual lifestyles ought to be created to suit individuals' personalities. The UVP tells us that no one person is more valuable than another, and yet, each is completely unique. So, *your* desired lifestyle won't be *my* desired lifestyle. There is no archetypal lifestyle for doctors, soldiers, authors, the middle class, or the working class. To believe so is a sure sign that you are raising cuckoos. For example, one author valuing excitement may have a proclivity for whitewater rafting, whereas another may prefer to nurture their desire for excitement as a spectator of ice hockey.

If you use neuro·ADAPT·ive Programming to create material wants—a red Ferrari, a trophy spouse, millions of dollars, a property portfolio, and so on—ahead of a fulfilling life, you'll be in danger of falling into at least two traps. The first is that of pursuing desires inspired by societal expectations (cuckoos), rather than desires that have emerged from within you. The peer pressure to be like everyone else, and to want what everyone else wants, is great indeed. The second is that going for the *stuff* before the lifestyle is the same as putting effect before cause. A cursory glance at the world at large will reveal the consequences of this. They include societies of peoples that, along with their financial wealth, are rife with severe depression, chronic illnesses, much dogma but little spirituality, greed, power mongering, disillusionment, broken relationships reflected in above 50 percent divorce rates, latchkey kids, illicit and prescribed drug abuse, and so on.

This is not for you! If it has been, it's time to change.

Knowing *how* you want to live is building your house on the rock and not on the sand. Once this foundation is in place, it becomes more apparent where and how the rooms need to be situated.

Your Automatic Guidance System

You've already poured the concrete for your foundation by creating your worthy ideal in chapter 4. Your worthy ideal is what supports your chosen lifestyle, and it is also how you choose to serve the world. It acts as an automatic guidance system to keep you on track.

I've often heard in business circles that even the most sophisticated NASA rocket is off-target 97 percent of the time it's in flight; yet, it still hits its target with pinpoint accuracy. While this may be an inaccurate statement, it is useful as a metaphor for continuing to pursue your worthy ideal when you yourself appear to be off-target.

The more automatic the guidance system, the more efficient it is. Note, then, the importance of the worthy ideal statement. While it can be used as a mantra, it should not be expected to create change by continued repetition alone. Instead, reviewing it either verbally or in writing can aid you in getting yourself back on track.

Consider this: A rocket traveling from earth would miss the moon by 4,169 miles (nearly twice its circumference) if it were off course by a mere 1 degree. With the same margin of error, it would miss the sun by 1.6 million miles and the nearest star system to our solar system, Alpha Centauri, by 441 billion miles. Living life without your own guidance system will have you just as off course; spiritually, mentally, and materially.

> A rocket traveling from earth would miss the moon by 4,169 miles (nearly twice its circumference) if it were off course by a mere 1 degree. Living life without your own guidance system will have you just as off course; spiritually, mentally, and materially.

It is important that your worthy ideal is consistent with the lifestyle you want. For example, if an aspect of your lifestyle is being at home with access to your grandchildren 24-7-365, you'd probably be unhappy being an author that regularly speaks in public all over the world. The inconsistency would be an indication that there's still a cuckoo in your nest. It could be in the lifestyle corner of the nest, or the worthy ideal corner. Either way, root it out with further introspection.

Choosing Your Vehicle

Just as your worthy ideal should support your lifestyle, the vehicle you choose to carry it out must support it. For example, if your worthy ideal is to be an architect, designing eco-friendly homes in depressed neighborhoods, you must decide between being an employee of a firm, a self-employed sole proprietor, a partnership with one or more other people, a corporation that employs other architects, and so on. This may seem extremely rudimentary—and it is. Nevertheless, I can share stories of painters who just wanted to paint, but found themselves hating life because they were doing the books, marketing, sales, and promotion as well as painting. Then, there's the bar owner who loved being *Mein Host*, spending as much time on the "other side of the bar" with his customers, but found that absentee staff meant that a twelve-hour shift on any given day was a luxury, and seven-day working weeks were the norm.

In the cases mentioned, the lack of initial visioneering and planning precluded each person from creating a structure in which the vehicle supported the worthy ideal, which in turn supported the desired lifestyle.

Your Fulfilling Life Action Assignment

1. Describe the value others will get from your worthy ideal. This will give you greater clarity.

2. List at least three things that pursuing your worthy ideal will bring, that you value above money.

3. Identify at least one cuckoo that you've been raising. Does it serve your worthy ideal?

    a. If yes: How can you leverage it?

    b. If no: How can you rid yourself of it?

CHAPTER TWELVE

neuro·ADAPT·ive Programming—Practice

Implementing neuro·ADAPT·ive Programming

Remember, your mortal self and the circumstances it finds itself in are the effects created by your immortal self. So, while the former imagines there to be a place and time somewhere "out there and then" in the future, when you might be, do, and have what you want, your immortal self doesn't recognize any such temporality. For it, there is only one eternal—*now*. That means when you claim to be, do, and have what you want, that claim can only be staked in the present. It is imperative, therefore, to declare, "I am what I would be, do, and have" and never, "I will be...."

Applying the Laws of Creation

When creating an entire lifestyle, you may wish to do so one ambition at a time. The key to getting the full benefit is to focus on initiating the causes that lead to the circumstances you want—and not the circumstances themselves. For example, an ideal life partner would be part of most people's ideal lifestyle. When attracting this person, your aim would be to first determine what *qualities* such a person would have—etiquette, lovingness, kindness, generosity, and so on—instead of the *features* such a person would have—brown hair, green eyes etc. I would also advise against being as specific as identifying a particular person, like John or Janet next door. Doing so is operating from the world of effects, not causes, and there's a good chance of adding to the already horrendous divorce statistics.

To implement neuro·ADAPT·ive Programming, you are going to be using the laws of creation from chapter 10. Let's recap how they work. First, you will be impregnating your subconscious mind with a conscious desire. This is the law of polarity in operation. Now, going back to the manifestation of your ideal life partner, ask yourself, "Do I have these qualities?" If not, then ask, "Do I have opposite, but complementary qualities?" The first of these two questions concerns the law of attraction, and the second, the law of repulsion: like attracts like; and opposites that are complementary also attract, like the north and south poles of magnets.

If you have neither the qualities you expect your ideal life partner to have, nor the opposite but complementary qualities, you need to develop whichever of these sets of qualities you think are most appropriate, in order for you to be attractive to that ideal person. For example, if you want to attract a life partner who is even-tempered, but you are angry much of the time, you may want to work on releasing that anger. Anger is neither like even-temperedness, nor is it a complementary opposite. Conversely, an idealist and a pragmatist could claim to have opposite but complementary qualities that might handsomely benefit a relationship between the two.

When you gain the necessary qualities, the energy you put out during your neuro-ADAPT-ive Programming sessions will have a more karmic effect. This energy is the cosmic power that you convert to personal power. Doing this work is very important; you cannot attract persons, experiences, or things that don't resonate with you. The work will change your vibrational resonance to make you the kind of person who attracts what you desire. So, here are some spiritual practices for real-world results.

Practices to Manage Causes

Journaling

Keeping a daily journal of your most prevalent positive and negative thoughts and words will help you to identify the habits that are serving you—and the ones that are not. By changing those patterns of thinking and talking, you will create new and better-serving causes.

Responsibility is 90 percent awareness and 10 percent action to create change. So, now that you know that journaling is a good idea, go the final 10 percent by actually *doing* it. I suggest keeping your journal handy so that you are more inclined to use it as a tool for change. Take it to bed to capture your dreams; take it on walks with you; make a note of anything your instincts tell you to; and, for the very best results, review your notes at the end of each day, identifying anything that strikes you as particularly significant. Once identified, decide what you are going to do about those significant points.

Notice your negative and positive activity about others as well as yourself. What you think and say about others, whether in their presence or not, affects you more than it does them. It is the karmic force at work, based on the unity of all things.

> *Responsibility is 90 percent awareness and 10 percent action*

Creating a Fulfilling Life Through Spiritual Growth

Positive Self-Talk

It is not enough to stop thinking about what you don't want in your life; physicists like to say that nature abhors a vacuum. The void created by *not* thinking about what you *don't* want is likely to be filled with more negativity, unless you consciously replace it with positivity. You will notice that this is the meaning of Matthew 12:43-45, especially when you substitute the words *idea* and *it* for the words *spirit* and *he*, respectively:

> "When an unclean spirit goes out of a man, he goes through dry places, seeking rest, and finds none. Then he says, 'I will return to my house from which I came.' And when he comes, he finds it empty, swept, and put in order. Then he goes and takes with him seven other spirits more wicked than himself, and they enter and dwell there; and the last state of that man is worse than the first."

Decide what it is that you *do* want to be saying about yourself. Make sure it's consistent with who you want to be and what you want to attract into your life. Create an affirmation that you can repeat to yourself throughout the day, especially in moments of doubt, fear, and confusion. We are warned against vain repetition, but when repeated with feeling, vision, and intention, your affirmation becomes very effective indeed. Be patient with yourself. Results may be speedy, but they are just as likely not to be. Finally, remember that this is part of the overall plan, rather than a cure-all.

Delete That Program

Many years ago, I attended a seminar by a guy called Jack Black (not the Jack Black of movie fame, but a renowned motivational speaker). One of the great bits of advice I got from him was to say "Delete that program" immediately upon thinking or saying something to myself, about myself, or about someone else that is not in harmony with who I want to be. To this day, I find this a most useful pattern interruption to get my thoughts, words, and deeds back on track. Thankfully, I find myself needing it less and less.

Meditation

The rise in popularity of meditation has brought about numerous variations on the theme. My personal preference is for silent meditation (without a mantra). Random thoughts (which can be likened to radio static) may come to mind during your meditation; resist the temptation to chase them away. The better you become at just observing them, then moving your mind on from them, the fewer you'll get. Your purpose is to *feel* your oneness with all of creation in general, and with spirit in particular. Remember the icy Arctic Ocean from chapter 7. If you are in everything and everything is in you, you can start to resonate spiritually with what you want to manifest in your life.

If you find it difficult to sit still for twenty to thirty minutes in silent meditation, start with five to ten minutes. If this is still unbearable, perhaps start with guided meditations that incorporate soothing music and are focused on manifesting a given quality such as love, harmony, joy, health, or success. Guided meditations themselves come in several variations—I particularly like those accompanied by soothing music and binaural beats. They are widely available and can be obtained from places like Google Play, the App Store, iTunes, YouTube, and various Internet sites.

A binaural beat is an illusion of sound created in the mind when two different sound frequencies are presented to the brain dichotically (one frequency through the right ear and a different frequency through the left ear, simultaneously). When this is done, the mind creates its own third frequency—the binaural beat—which is equal to the difference between the two "real" frequencies. Researchers have proven that by creating a binaural beat at four to eight hertz—a *theta* frequency—the brain is triggered to resonate at that same frequency, quickly and easily guiding your mind into brainwave activity in the theta state. The same can be done to guide brainwave activity at the other four frequencies: *gamma*, *beta*, *alpha*, and *delta*.

The significance of theta binaural beat brainwave activity is that it is consistent with the brainwave activity which is apparent during the meditation of one who is accomplished in the practice. Theta waves are known to stimulate creativity, emotional connection, intuition, and relaxation.

Of course, there are also forms of moving meditation like yoga, *tai chi*, *qi gong*, and even walking and jogging. Although moving meditations do not involve stilling the body, what remains most important is creating a space to experience divine presence. Because the movements involved in these types of meditation are so rhythmic, they become autonomic (unconscious). This allows your conscious mind to relax enough to enable intuitive insights to flow through from your subconscious.

Contemplation

Contemplation is being attentive to the present moment, regardless of what you are contemplating. It includes looking thoughtfully at something for a while or thinking deeply about a challenge, puzzle, or problem. It also includes concentrating on spiritual matters, like the nature of the Creator, your relationship with It, and your

> *When I look in the mirror through my own eyes and declare who I am, there comes a point when it's no longer a wish hoped for, but a declaration of truth.*

unity with other people and nature. It is best done in peaceful, natural surroundings. Remain present. If your mind wanders to past regrets or future concerns, bring it back to the present by focusing on what's immediately around you: birds, trees, landscapes—whatever you have available. Feel your connection with these things from the still silent place within.

The Value of Spiritual Practices

As a child, I remember quizzing a cousin about a place where she had vacationed with her family. My questions were so incessant that after a while she said, "I can't explain it any better, you just had to be there." It's the same with these practices. My telling you about them isn't enough; you have to engage in them. That being said, what follows are examples of successful applications of the practices from my personal experience.

Journaling

My book, *Embracing Failure: Your Key to Success* began as a journal. Its initial purpose was to help me understand why my first business had failed so miserably. During the process of journaling, the number and quality of epiphanies that rose from the pages I was writing, brought my attention to the idea that what I was writing should be shared with others who had suffered a failure like mine, and had then wanted to turn it around.

Positive Self-Talk

I know beyond doubt that my affirmations (which include "delete that program") have helped shape who I am and what I have achieved. When I look in the mirror through my own eyes and declare who I am, there comes a point when it's no longer a wish hoped for, but a declaration of truth. That's when I know my subconscious has said, "Thank you. I've got this. I'll take it from here." Becoming a bestselling author is an example of this.

Meditation

Many of the ideas in need of refining for this book, and the questions that required answering, were satisfied during periods of meditation and contemplation. One such question was how to vividly demonstrate the way in which the forces of creation all work together as a single harmonious arrangement. While meditating one morning, the metaphor of the orbiting planet that I used toward the end of chapter 10 was given to me. Hand on heart, I can say that meditation is the single most important activity I do on a daily basis.

As well as gaining access to subconscious inspiration, the more you practice meditation, the more you can bring the peace you experience during meditation into your mundane world, in order to enjoy better clarity of thought and increased certainty of actions. The physical and mental health benefits of meditation are well documented in numerous studies worldwide. They include reduced blood pressure, a strengthened immune response, improved physical and emotional responses to stress, reduced anxiety, relief from fibromyalgia symptoms, and even relief from the symptoms of psoriasis.

The scientific efficacy of meditation is so proven that universities such as Emory University School of Medicine in Atlanta, Georgia, offer courses in it.

Contemplation

I scarcely go for a walk without bringing a notepad and pen, or an audio recorder. The daily practice of taking a long walk in natural surroundings can prove extremely beneficial for problem solving and stress reduction. It needs to be for no other reason than to forget the cares of the workplace and the world; nonetheless, you'll return to your office a better person and a more productive one.

Remaining present can open up opportunities for intuitive insights to flow through from your subconscious mind. I recall someone dear to me sharing one such moment of wisdom from a period of contemplation. Her teenage son was becoming too dependent on her and she didn't know how to handle his reluctance to grow up. While on a walk in the woods, she noticed a bird pushing its chick out of the nest. While she didn't go home and send her son packing, she was clear that enabling him was disempowering him. So, no matter how emotionally tormenting letting go was for her, she knew she had to.

Sometimes, a thought gained in meditation is expanded upon while contemplating, and vice versa. As I meditated one day, the puzzlement of a universe that is expanding forever came to mind. Later that day, during my contemplation, the thought developed. This is what I wrote in my journal:

Is the universe really expanding, or is expansion a figment of our limited senses and mind?

Intellectually, we can talk about infinity, but conceptually, we cannot grasp it. To do so would be to limit the limitless. To prove the point, let's imagine an infinitely large equilateral triangle. Where do the points of such a triangle meet in spacetime? If they do meet, the infinite triangle cannot be static. If it is static, it can be measured and, therefore, is not infinite. The triangle, then, must be forever expanding. If it is expanding, it is expanding toward an unattainable infinity; for stopping expanding is to become limited.

Infinity, then, is a phenomenon that has to be outside of spacetime—eternal.

Is what we observe as an expanding universe really an infinity that our obtuse five senses and mind cannot grasp? The universe is of time and space, and also a creation—not a cause. If there is to be an infinity, it has to be First Cause; and, as such, encompass all that is. Everything has to be an expression of it; otherwise, it is not infinite. This description fits well with what some of us refer to as the Creator.

The universe, as we know it, is a material expression of Infinity—the Creator—and so, as with the concept of the infinite equilateral triangle, our five senses and mind perceive it as expanding, whether it is or is not.

Now, whether this is genius or gibberish is beside the point. The point is that I expand my range of thinking through these two disciplines. The box that would otherwise limit my thinking is discarded.

Engaging in these practices is, to persons aspiring to better their lives, akin to woodsmen sharpening their axes: invaluable.

The Nine Acts of neuro·ADAPT·ive Programming

This is where you'll employ the worthy ideal statement you developed in chapter 5, as the basis for supercharging the creation of your fulfilling life using neuro·ADAPT·ive Programming. My intention is not to build your lifestyle for you, but to demonstrate how neuro·ADAPT·ive Programming works. Simplicity is best when doing so. Let us therefore go through the process of creating a dream home to demonstrate exactly that.

Neuro·ADAPT·ive Programming allows you to dream your life, then live your dream on demand. This is exactly how Vincent van Gogh created his masterpieces. He once said:

> *"I dream my painting, and then I paint my dream."*

I'm using a broad definition of the word *dream*, which includes any activity of your conscious mind that you use to impress your desires upon your subconscious mind.

When describing what neuro·ADAPT·ive Programming is in chapter 2, I said that "...emotions are the conduit along which beliefs are transmitted to the subconscious mind." The stronger your emotions, the greater their ability to affect your subconscious mind. There is no lasting change without affecting the subconscious. Needless to say, then, that the stronger the positive emotions you can apply to the assumption of achieving your worthy ideal, the likelier the ideal is to materialize.

What you are aiming for in your neuro·ADAPT·ive Programming sessions, is a crystal-clear picture of the outcome you want with a statement of that picture, and a highly emotional mental experience of achieving that outcome.

Act 1—Your Screenplay

Create a short script that you will enact as a theater production; one that does not feel like theater, but real life—similar to a dream you imagine to be real until you awake from sleep. It is important that your play has another person with whom you will communicate. Keep the script simple. For example, it may be as simple as:

> *neuro·ADAPT·ive Programming allows you to dream your life, then live your dream on demand.*

OTHER PERSON: *"Congratulations. Here's the key to your new home."*

YOU: *"Thank you!"*

When creating an entire lifestyle, the complexity is increased. However, be sure that your play is simple enough to perform within a reasonable timeframe. If you work twelve hours a day, homeschool the kids, and are also the home help for an elderly parent, you likely won't have two hours a day for creation. Similarly, if you aren't used to a practice involving introspective quiet time, as little as ten minutes may be challenging. Regardless of your circumstances, aim for a play that is high in *quality*, rather than *quantity*. Beware not to make any unfamiliarity with introspective quiet time an excuse to do nothing.

Act 2—Sensualize

As you go through your play, don't just visualize. Use all of your spiritual sensory perception. As well as seeing the carnations, you must smell them. You're going to feel yourself saying, *"Thank you!"* and feel the press of the other person's handshake as you speak. If you were chewing gum before receiving the key to your new home, taste the freshness of the mint flavor in your mouth. Apart from the dialogue between you and the other person, what other sounds are there? The more of you that can be engaged in the play, the greater the intensity and variety of emotions you can bring to bear. The more deeply you can embody those emotions as feelings, the stronger are the creative forces working for you. And, of course, be sure to only experience positive emotions and feelings.

Act 3—The Scene

Set the scene. Make sure that your sensualized play is

always performed on the same set. Sensualize exactly the same things in the scene every time. If the other person is wearing a gray suit, have them always wearing a gray suit. If there is a vase with carnations, always visualize the same vase with carnations, and so on.

Act 4—See Through Your Eyes

Do not see *with* your eyes. Instead, see *through* your eyes. In the former case, you are an observer *of* your play. In the latter case, you are the lead actor *in* your play. For example, if you are face-to-face with the other person, you shouldn't be able to see either your back or theirs; just what is in front of you. If you are seeing your back, you are seeing with your eyes as an observer. If mastering the skill of seeing through your eyes doesn't come easily to you, persist; you just need to strengthen that spiritual muscle. Know that you can if you really want to. Being able to see through your eyes is extremely important.

Act 5—Be Present

Be convinced that this home closing is happening right here, right now, and not some other place at some future time. "Right here" could be thousands of miles away from wherever you are physically, during the play. If you are sensualizing in, say, Cheyenne, Wyoming, and the keys are being handed over in Los Angeles, California, you must be mentally in Los Angeles, California, right now, during the sensualization. This is as important a point as seeing *through* your eyes. What you want is not in the future, but within you *now*. In other words, whatever you want is already yours...IF you really believe it to be. Again, your subconscious mind does not recognize temporality, so to include a notion of "now and then" will weaken the creative process.

Act 6—Timing

You can do this exercise at any time of the day. The optimum times, though, are as you awake from sleep and just before going to sleep—especially the latter. At these times, your brainwave activity is closer to the slower alpha and theta states. The more you can bypass the conscious mind for this sensualization, the better.

Act 7—Know it Is Done

This is where you must rely on your faith; it's also a great test of your faith. Know that what you are asking for is what you will get. There is a body-mind parallel to this spiritual alchemy of seeing what you first believe—the scotoma (or blind spot) near the center of the visual field. Some psychological processes provide information from surrounding detail, and from the other eye, to see what (isn't there, but that) we believe is there:

> *"[O]f this personal vision, a worldview is born and an entire life lived.... These meanings become difficult to change because we similarly believe that we really see them rather than create them."*
>
> —**Ellyn Kaschak, PhD, psychology**

In a similar manner to the scotoma effect, spiritually, the subconscious mind will create the circumstances of your life. It does so by adding whatever is required to what you have already provided in your spiritual practices with sufficient faith and emotion. It will believe that it really sees the circumstances rather than creating them.

As incredible as this faculty is, do not omit the vital component of action. If you are in the desert and you have prayed (sensualized) for rain to fill water bottles, you'd better make sure you have water bottles to fill. This active mode represents the ACE components of faith discussed

> *If you are in the desert and you have prayed (sensualized) for rain to fill water bottles, you'd better make sure you have water bottles to fill.*

in chapter 9. Taking action in the material world is as much a part of the process of creation as the spiritual practices that initiate its causes.

While causes, which we discussed earlier as being spiritual, express themselves through our actions and manifest circumstances, an additional benefit of our actions is the reinforcement of our spiritual being. We see evidence of this in the autonomic responses of experienced drivers in avoiding automobile accidents, and in the autonomic reflexes of highly skilled athletes. In other words, repeated actions strengthen spiritual "muscle". Accordingly, meaningful actions aid in the purposeful subconscious management of your life, and so deter its predisposition to controlling your life using the detrimental, repressed memories embedded therein.

Act 8—Gestation

There will usually be some gestation period between spiritual cause and material effect. It takes nine months of pregnancy to give birth to a child; it takes about forty-five minutes for yeast to raise dough. In other words, an email announcing that the seller has accepted your price and terms for your dream home may not hit your inbox the day after your first sensualization.

While material effects are subject to linear time and have an apparent time period for manifestation, there is no movement of time in the spiritual world; only restructured consciousness. Levels of consciousness may be seen as degrees of awareness progressing toward divine perfection. An increase in awareness is not something that you can force. To grasp this concept, imagine yourself as a point of individual awareness within the infinity of universal consciousness, and as being inseparable from it. As you experience spiritual growth, universal consciousness pulls you upward, so to speak, to occupy a level that is commensurate with your growth. In this way, you assume the *states* of the things you want to be, do, and have, be they physical, like a home; intellectual, like knowledge; or emotional, like joy (though not the fleeting kind).

Act 9—Don't Micromanage Your Subconscious

Allow your subconscious mind to determine the *how* part of this process. For example, don't be fixated on the dream home coming from a particular source: a real estate agent you know, a "For sale by owner" sign, a foreclosure, an auction, or whatever. Your responsibility is to determine what you want (and, to some degree, by when you want it, without making the *when* too hard and fast). Your subconscious will take it from there. This is observance of the advice to "let go and let God."

So, What Now?

These nine acts, then, comprise the neuro·ADAPT·ive Programming process. At this point I'm reminded of G. K. Chesterton's counsel that "...the Christian ideal has not been tried and found wanting. It has been found difficult; and left untried."

— G. K. Chesterton, *What's Wrong With the World*

You can apply this same reasoning to neuro·ADAPT·ive Programming. For *it* to work for *you*, *you* have to work *it*.

By first impregnating your subconscious mind with conscious desire, you are using the law of polarity, from which the laws of attraction, repulsion, and karma are set in motion to create the lifestyle you desire. The extent to which you are faithful to the process is the extent to which it will be faithful to you. This is a specific application of the general principle that states that nature will obey you to the exact proportion that you obey nature.

Your Fulfilling Life Action Assignment

1. Decide what spiritual practices you are going to use regularly. Start using them right away.
2. Complete Acts 1 through 9 for your neuro·ADAPT·ive Programming sessions.
3. Decide what times of day you will use neuro·ADAPT·ive Programming, then start using it within one day of finishing the book.

Summary

Throughout this book we have broached the subject of spirituality. The purpose of this discussion has not been to confer sainthood upon you, but for you to better understand who you are, what you want, and how to get it so that it lasts.

When experiencing life primarily from the body-mind realms, we are the products of heredity and environment. Our fate is seemingly dependent on the luck of the draw—to whom we are born and where we are raised. Influences beyond our control blow us here and there. Our actions are determined by a set of (sometimes superficial) beliefs, adopted from others, which are scarcely grounded in knowledge. Many of these beliefs have been passed on for generations and we have accepted them without question.

Science would have us believe that the entirety of life is that which can be observed and measured in the material world, even when the thoughts that produce its theories cannot be observed, measured, or sourced in that world. Some religious interpretations of spirit have us worshipping false gods who are equally adept at inflicting evil as they are at dispensing good. Philosophies come and go with the tides of cultural change.

Basing life on the premises of science, religion, or philosophy creates a gap between our individual personal reality and spiritual truth. The gap is only narrowed when we embrace the spiritual realm of life, which is only experienced when the body is still and the mind silent. It is from this latter realm that we receive eternal truths like $1 + 1 = 2$ and the integrity of perfect shapes like the circle, which exist independent of the existence of humankind, or any material phenomenon. The more we narrow the gap between our individual personal reality and spiritual truth, the more capable we are of creating a fulfilling life.

Our lives are harmonized when we experience it from all three realms, allowing the divine perfection of the spiritual realm to be the cause of effects experienced in the other two. We can liken a life experienced from all three realms to gold prospecting. The best prospectors will have an assortment of necessary physical equipment: a drywasher, sluice box, dredge, pans, etc.; a well-prepared mind from education and experience of where to find nuggets; and, last but by no means least, the spiritual sixth sense drawing them toward the gold. It is said that the old prospector could just *smell* gold.

The more we experience life as spirit, the more we develop our *smell* for the fulfilling life we want, overcoming the uncertainty of outcomes offered by reliance on our heredity and environment alone. We must still the body and quiet the mind on a regular basis to receive guidance from within.

Once we have clarity about what makes for a fulfilling life, we can enhance the likelihood of getting it by employing neuro-ADAPT-ive programming.

Knowingly or not, you now find yourself at a crossroads. One direction leads you to the path that most with some spiritual acumen take: using their spiritual knowledge exclusively to satisfy their material appetites. Suffice it to say, there is no security or peace of mind in anything of this perishable, material world of heredity and environment.

The other way is a path taken by a small minority. It is the road less traveled, leading to a life dedicated to serving spirit, which does not mean becoming a clergyperson or anything of the sort. It does, however, mean becoming one whose life is dedicated to serving others in total confidence and reliance that your complete well-being is catered for by spirit. This reliance requires an understanding that spirit is cause, and all that is body-mind is effect.

The road less traveled is the steeper path, leading to the highest peaks with the most beautiful vistas. When we reach the summit:

"Instead of repeated efforts to make good come to us, our every good unfolds to view from the depths of our own being without conscious effort, either physical or mental. We are no longer dependent on person or circumstances, nor even on our personal effort. Spiritual illumination enables us to relax our personal efforts and rely more and more on Divinity unfolding and revealing Itself to us as us."

—Joel Goldsmith, **The Infinite Way**

The essential reasons for it being the road less traveled are the same as those encountered in chapter 5, under the subheading *The Three Devils You Must Avoid: Ignorance, Disbelief, and Fear.* Working on yourself to overcome these is the difficult path, indeed.

Regardless of which of the two paths you decide to take, when you face the final curtain, you can say along with Frank Sinatra:

"I did it my way."

www.ingramcontent.com/pod-product-compliance
Lightning Source LLC
Chambersburg PA
CBHW070559010526
44118CB00012B/1375